ENGAGE THE BRAIN

GAMEs

MARCIA L. TATE

CORWIN PRESS
Classroom

For information:

Corwin Press
A SAGE Company
2455 Teller Road
Thousand Oaks, California 91320
CorwinPress.com

SAGE, Ltd.
1 Oliver's Yard
55 City Road
London EC1Y 1SP
United Kingdom

SAGE India Pvt. Ltd.
B 1/I 1 Mohan Cooperative
Industrial Area
Mathura Road, New Delhi
India 110 044

SAGE Asia-Pacific Pvt. Ltd.
33 Pekin Street #02-01
Far East Square
Singapore 048763

Printed in the United States of America.

ISBN: 978-1-4129-5930-8

This book is printed on acid-free paper.

08 09 10 11 12 10 9 8 7 6 5 4 3 2 1

Executive Editor: Kathleen Hex
Managing Developmental Editor: Christine Hood
Editorial Assistant: Anne O'Dell
Developmental Writer: Vicky Shiotsu
Developmental Editor: Susan Hodges
Proofreader: Mary Barbosa
Art Director: Anthony D. Paular
Design Project Manager: Jeffrey Stith
Cover Designers: Lisa Miller and Monique Hahn
Illustrator: Corbin Hillam
Cover Illustrator: Jane Yamada
Design Consultant: The Development Source

GRADE 3

TABLE OF CONTENTS

Connections to Standards

This chart shows the national academic standards covered in each chapter.

LANGUAGE ARTS	Standards are covered on pages
Apply a wide range of strategies to comprehend, interpret, evaluate, and appreciate texts. Draw on prior experience, interactions with other readers and writers, knowledge of word meaning and of other texts, word identification strategies, and understanding of textual features (e.g., sound-letter correspondence, sentence structure, context, graphics).	11, 13, 18
Adjust the use of spoken, written, and visual language (e.g., conventions, style, vocabulary) to communicate effectively with a variety of audiences and for different purposes.	16
Apply knowledge of language structure, language conventions (e.g., spelling and punctuation), media techniques, figurative language, and genre to create, critique, and discuss print and nonprint texts.	9, 22
Conduct research on issues and interests by generating ideas and questions, and by posing problems. Gather, evaluate, and synthesize data from a variety of sources (e.g., print and nonprint texts, artifacts, people) to communicate discoveries in ways that suit the purpose and audience.	26
Use spoken, written, and visual language to accomplish a purpose (e.g., for learning, enjoyment, persuasion, and the exchange of information).	22

MATHEMATICS	Standards are covered on pages
Number and Operations—Understand numbers, ways of representing numbers, relationships among numbers, and number systems.	28
Number and Operations—Understand meanings of operations and how they relate to one another.	28, 31
Number and Operations—Compute fluently and make reasonable estimates.	31, 33
Algebra—Understand patterns, relations, and functions.	36
Algebra—Represent and analyze mathematical situations and structures using algebraic symbols.	36
Geometry—Analyze characteristics and properties of two- and three-dimensional geometric shapes, and develop mathematical arguments about geometric relationships.	39, 41
Geometry—Use visualization, spatial reasoning, and geometric modeling to solve problems.	39

Measurement—Understand measurable attributes of objects and the units, systems, and processes of measurement.	43
Measurement—Apply appropriate techniques, tools, and formulas to determine measurements.	43
Data Analysis and Probability—Select and use appropriate statistical methods to analyze data.	45

SCIENCE	Standards are covered on pages
Physical Science—Understand position and motion of objects.	47
Physical Science—Understand light, heat, electricity, and magnetism.	49
Life Science—Understand characteristics of organisms.	51
Life Science—Understand organisms and environments.	54
Earth and Space Science—Understand properties of earth materials.	56
Earth and Space Science—Identify objects in the sky.	59, 62
Earth and Space Science—Understand changes in the earth and sky.	62

SOCIAL STUDIES	Standards are covered on pages
Understand culture and cultural diversity.	64
Understand the interactions among people, places, and environments.	67
Understand how people create and change structures of power, authority, and governance.	74
Understand how people organize for the production, distribution, and consumption of goods and services.	76
Understand relationships among science, technology, and society.	76, 78
Understand the ideals, principles, and practices of citizenship in a democratic republic.	71

Introduction

An ancient Chinese proverb claims: "Tell me, I forget. Show me, I remember. Involve me, I understand." This timeless saying illuminates what all educators should know: Unless students are involved and actively engaged in learning, true learning rarely occurs.

The latest brain research reveals that both the right and left hemispheres of the brain should be engaged in the learning process. This is important because the hemispheres talk to one another over the corpus callosum, the structure that connects them. No strategies are better designed for promoting communication between the hemispheres than games. Play speeds up the brain's maturation process because it involves the built-in processes of challenge, novelty, feedback, coherence, and time. In addition, games are fun—and fun is an important component of learning. Students of all ages learn best when they enjoy the process. Therefore, it makes sense to incorporate games into the curriculum to stimulate and reinforce learning.

How to Use This Book

The activities in this book cover the content areas and are designed using strategies that actively engage the brain. To ensure that students get the most out of each lesson, activities are presented in the way the brain learns best: focus activity, modeling, guided practice, check for understanding, independent practice, and closing. Go through each step to ensure that students will be fully engaged in the concept being taught and understand its purpose and meaning.

Each game is designed so that students can make important connections between related concepts. You will find games that encourage students to apply their learning and practice skills, games that review and reinforce concepts, games that promote strategy planning and critical thinking, and more! Students will enjoy playing variations of classic games such as relay races, Go Fish, Hot Potato, Tic-Tac-Toe, scavenger hunts, and Bingo. In addition, many of the games can be adapted for play with student pairs, small groups, or the entire class.

These brain-compatible activities are sure to engage and motivate every student's brain in your classroom! Watch your students change from passive to active learners as they process game experiences into learning that is not only fun but also remembered for a lifetime.

Put It Into Practice

Lecture and repetitive worksheets have long been the traditional method of delivering knowledge and reinforcing learning. While some higher-achieving students may engage in this type of learning, educators now know that actively engaging students' brains is not a luxury, but a necessity if students are truly to acquire and retain content, not only for tests but for life.

The 1990s were dubbed the Decade of the Brain because millions of dollars were spent on brain research. Educators today should know more about how students learn than ever before. Learning styles theories that call for student engagement have been proposed for decades, as evidenced by research such as Howard Gardner's theory of multiple intelligences (1983), Bernice McCarthy's 4MAT Model (1990), and VAKT (visual, auditory, kinesthetic, tactile) learning styles theories.

I have identified 20 strategies that, according to brain research and learning styles theories, appear to correlate with the way the brain learns best. I have observed hundreds of teachers—regular education, special education, and gifted. Regardless of the classification or grade level of the students, exemplary teachers consistently use these 20 strategies to deliver memorable classroom instruction and help their students understand and retain vast amounts of content.

These 20 brain-based instructional strategies include the following:

1. Brainstorming and Discussion

2. Drawing and Artwork

3. Field Trips

4. Games

5. Graphic Organizers, Semantic Maps, and Word Webs

6. Humor

7. Manipulatives, Experiments, Labs, and Models

8. Metaphors, Analogies, and Similes

9. Mnemonic Devices

10. Movement

11. Music, Rhythm, Rhyme, and Rap

12. Project-based and Problem-based Instruction

13. Reciprocal Teaching and Cooperative Learning

14. Role Play, Drama, Pantomime, Charades

15. Storytelling

16. Technology

17. Visualization and Guided Imagery

18. Visuals

19. Work Study and Apprenticeships

20. Writing and Journals

This book features Instructional Strategy 4: Games. Through play, people fulfill the body's need to express emotions, to bond with others socially, and to explore new learning with challenge, feedback, and success (Beyers, 1998).

Lessons can be drudgery when students are expected to learn facts by drill. Worksheets and flashcards offer students little opportunity for engagement. However, reviewing information in a game format will motivate and engage even the most reluctant learners. The mechanisms involved when students are playing a game are just as cognitive as when students are doing math seatwork (Bjorkland & Brown, 1998). When students play games, they engage in the most basic level of active processing—creative rehearsal (Caine & Caine, 1994).

Play is fun with a purpose. It fulfills our need to express emotions, bond with others socially, and explore new learning with challenge, feedback, and success (Beyers, 1998). A well-designed game offers students the optimal amount of challenge. It is motivating but never frustrating. Similarly, students need feedback on their performance, and such feedback is an intrinsic part of every game. As students play, they reveal what they have learned and what they do not yet understand. In the process, games also provide feedback for the teacher. Finally, games let students experience success. They provide a safe, unthreatening environment in which everyone can win.

Games become more even meaningful and motivating when students are involved in constructing them (Wolfe, 2001). Many of the activities in this book provide students with a game format they can use to develop their own challenging games. Such activities require students to actively engage with the content and to present what they know in new ways.

These memorable strategies help students make sense of learning by focusing on the ways the brain learns best. Fully supported by the latest brain research, Tate's strategies provide the tools you need to boost motivation, energy, and most important, the academic achievement of your students.

978-1-4129-5930-8

CHAPTER 1

Language Arts

Spelling Tic-Tac-Toe

Objective
Students will practice spelling words.

Materials
- writing paper
- pencils

Activities that encourage visualization of words or word parts help students develop effective spelling strategies. This twist on the game *Tic-Tac-Toe* adds excitement to an otherwise ordinary spelling task.

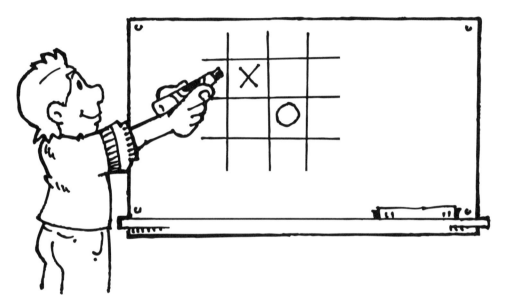

1. Ask students if they know how to play Tic-Tac-Toe. Then draw a 3 x 3 grid on the board, and call on two volunteers to demonstrate the game for the class. Point out that the winner is the first player to get three marks in a vertical, horizontal, or diagonal row.

2. Tell students that they will be playing a special Tic-Tac-Toe game to review their spelling words. Then divide the class into two teams, and designate one team as X and one team as O. Give each team writing paper and pencils.

3. Draw a 4 x 4 grid on the board. Explain and model the rules of the game.
   a. Give the first team a word to spell. Team members can talk together and discuss the correct spelling of the word. They may also practice writing the word on paper.
   b. One player spells the word aloud. If the answer is correct, the player writes an X on the game board.

c. If the answer is not correct, the other team has a chance to answer. (If both teams answer incorrectly, the class works with you to sound out the word, syllable by syllable, while you write the word on the board.)

d. Play continues with a new spelling word. The game ends when one team marks a row of Xs or Os horizontally, vertically, or diagonally, or all of the spaces of the grid are filled.

e. At the end of the game, teams earn points as follows: one point for three in a row and two points for four in a row. The team with the most points wins the game.

4. Play a practice round to make sure students understand how to play. Then begin a real game.

5. Let the class help you add up the scores for each team to determine the winner. In the example shown below, Team 1 scored four points for one horizontal row of four Xs, one vertical row of three Xs, and one diagonal row of three Xs. Team 2 also scored four points for one horizontal row of three Os, two vertical rows of three Os, and one diagonal row of three Os.

6. As a follow-up, discuss the following questions to help students evaluate their learning:
   - *How does writing a word on paper help you determine the correct spelling?*
   - *Why is it helpful to break a word into syllables when you are trying to spell it?*
       - *Try to "see" the word in your mind as you spell it. How can doing this help your spelling?*

Extended Learning
Have students play a Tic-Tac-Toe game as they solve math problems, give definitions for vocabulary words, answer questions about a science topic, or perform other tasks that review skills and concepts.

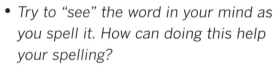

X	X	X	X
X	X	O	O
X	O	O	O
O	X	O	O

Vocabulary Grab Bag

Objective

Students will review vocabulary terms and generate sentences that use them.

Students need stimulating activities to help them learn and retain new vocabulary. In this challenging game, teams use two vocabulary words at a time to create sentences. By working cooperatively, students help one another review the meanings of words and generate sentences that illustrate proper word usage.

Materials
- 2 paper bags
- 30 to 40 word cards
- clock or watch with second hand

1. Spark students' interest in the game by writing on the board six vocabulary words that the class has recently learned. For example, if students have been reading E. B. White's *Stuart Little*, you might write words such as *belittle, annoyed, shrill, exasperated, gloomy,* and *thwarts*. Ask the class to briefly explain each word.

2. Next, tell students that you are going to give them an extra challenge. Underline two of the words and ask if anyone can quickly come up with a sentence that includes both words. Let two or three volunteers share their ideas with the class. Repeat the procedure with the remaining four words.

3. Tell students that they will be creating sentences for other pairs of vocabulary words, but that they will be working in teams. Then divide the class into four teams, and instruct each team to gather in a designated area of the room.

4. Place 15 to 20 word cards in each of two paper bags. Place the bags on a table or a desk at the front of the room. Then explain and model how to play the game.

   a. A player from the first team draws a word card from each bag and shows the cards to his or her team.

   b. The team has 30 seconds to think of a sentence that includes both words and say the sentence aloud. If the team answers correctly, they keep the cards. If the answer is not correct, the player returns the cards to the bags.

   c. The game continues with players from the other teams taking turns drawing cards and saying a sentence.

   d. At the end of the game, teams count their cards. The team with the most cards wins.

5. Draw two word cards and use them in a sentence. Ask the class to identify if you have used the words correctly. Do this several times to check for understanding. Then begin the game.

6. After the game, discuss any words that students found difficult. Review the meanings of the words, and write sentences on the board to show the words in context.

belittle shrill gloomy
annoyed exasperated thwarts

Variation of the Game

At the beginning of the game, give pencils and sheets of paper to each team. When it is a team's turn to think of a sentence, have one team member write the sentence instead of saying it aloud. (Extend the 30 seconds allotted in the original game to one minute.) After the game, have students illustrate the sentences generated by their teams.

978-1-4129-5930-8

Syllable Detectives

Objective

Students will read words and identify the number of syllables in each word.

Materials
- Syllable Detectives reproducible
- reading materials (e.g., books, magazines, newspapers)

In order to decode and read an unfamiliar word, students must be able to break it apart into different "chunks" of sound. Each chunk, or syllable, contains one vowel sound. In this game, students review the concept of syllables and look for words that have up to five syllables.

1. Get students ready to become "syllable detectives." Divide the class into pairs, and have partners face each other. Write the word *player* on the board, and instruct students to slowly say the word. Ask how many different mouth movements they made. *(two)* Tell students that the word *player* has two syllables. Explain that when they say a word, the number of movements their mouth makes indicates the number of syllables, or vowel sounds, in the word.

2. Write the following words on the board: *plant, animal, raincoat, photocopier, community, tree, beautiful*. Have students face their partners and slowly say each word. Ask students to observe the number of mouth movements their partners make for each word.

3. Discuss the number of syllables in each word. Guide the class to understand that the number of syllables matches the number of vowel sounds that are *heard*, not vowel letters that are *seen*. For example, explain that even though the word *raincoat* has four vowels, it has two syllables because only two vowel sounds—long *a* and long *o*—are heard.

4. Tell students that they will be playing a game called Syllable Detectives. Explain that they will be working with their partners to "hunt" for words that have varying numbers of syllables. At the end of the game, they will score points for each word they find.

5. Give each pair of students a copy of the **Syllable Detectives reproducible (page 15)** and books, magazines, and other reading materials. Then explain and model the rules of the game.
   a. Partners look through the reading materials for examples of words with one to five syllables.

b. Players write each word in the correct column of their reproducible. They may write up to five words per column.

c. After a given amount of time, players tally their score using the point system at the bottom of the reproducible. The pair with the most points wins.

6. Model finding words in the reading materials. Say each word slowly, and ask volunteers to identify the number of syllables. Ask in which column the word belongs on the reproducible. Answer any questions, and then have students play independently.

7. As students play, check that they are correctly identifying the number of syllables. If students have difficulty determining the number of syllables in a word, have them face their partner and say the word slowly, counting the number of movements their mouth makes. Instruct them to hold their hand under their chin and count the number of times their jaw moves.

8. As a follow-up, ask students to share some words they found. Write the words on the board and challenge the class to identify the number of syllables.

Extended Learning

Make a chart on butcher paper similar to that on the Syllable Detectives reproducible. Let students take turns filling in the chart with words from their lists. Afterward, discuss the following questions:

- *Which word is the longest?*

- *Which word has the most vowels?*

- *Which word is the most interesting?*

- *Which words have more vowels than syllables?*

Syllable Detectives

Directions: Find words to write in the columns below. Look in books, magazines, or newspapers. Write up to five words per column. Then total your points.

1 Syllable	2 Syllables	3 Syllables	4 Syllables	5 Syllables
made	carpet	expected	organizer	opportunity
say	after	government	transportation	investigation
week	Tuesday	surprising	affordable	
of	stories	understand	identify	
least	author	computer	macaroni	

1-syllable words (1 point each): _5_   4-syllable words (4 points each): _20_

2-syllable words (2 points each): _10_   5-syllable words (5 points each): _10_

3-syllable words (3 points each): _15_   **Total Number of Points:** _60_

978-1-4129-5930-8

Name _____ Date _____

Syllable Detectives

Directions: Find words to write in the columns below. Look in books, magazines, or newspapers. Write up to five words per column. Then total your points.

1 Syllable	2 Syllables	3 Syllables	4 Syllables	5 Syllables

1-syllable words (1 point each): _____

2-syllable words (2 points each): _____

3-syllable words (3 points each): _____

4-syllable words (4 points each): _____

5-syllable words (5 points each): _____

Total Number of Points: _____

Synonym Partners

Materials
- chart paper
- index cards (20 per student)
- envelopes

Objective
Students will identify and match pairs of synonyms.

A varied vocabulary strengthens a student's ability to communicate clearly and effectively. This game builds vocabulary skills and reinforces an awareness of synonyms.

1. Get students warmed up for this game by writing on the board: *An elephant is big.* Underline the word *big.* Have students read the sentence aloud. Next, ask the class to suggest other words that have the same meaning as *big* and write them on the board. Tell the class that these words are *synonyms.* Explain that synonyms are words that have the same, or almost the same, meaning. Then replace *big* in the sentence with *enormous.* Call on a student to read the sentence aloud. Tell the class that synonyms can make writing more vivid and interesting.

2. Work with the class to create a list of at least 12 pairs of synonyms. (If students suggest three or more words that are synonyms, include the extra words as well.) Write the words on chart paper. See the word box for suggestions.

Synonyms	
afraid, fearful, scared	look, gaze, stare
begin, start	mad, angry, furious
bright, shiny, dazzling	pretty, lovely, beautiful
cold, chilly	shout, yell, scream
easy, simple	small, little, tiny, wee
exciting, thrilling	tired, weary, exhausted
fast, quick, speedy	toss, throw, pitch
happy, glad, joyful	wet, moist, damp

3. Tell students that they will use these synonyms to make a card game similar to Go Fish. Give each student 20 index cards on which to write ten pairs of synonyms. They can also think of their own synonyms.

4. Call on two students to help you model the game as you explain the rules.
   a. Players combine their word cards. One player shuffles the cards, deals six cards to each player, and places the remaining cards facedown in a pile.

b. Players look at their cards, remove any matching pairs of synonyms, and place them faceup on the table. (If by chance a player has three words that match—that is, both players created word cards using the same pair of synonyms—then only two of the three cards are used.)

c. Players take turns asking each other for a synonym that matches a word card in their hand. If there is a match, the player takes the card from the other player and lays down the matching pair. If not, the player must "go fish" and draw a card from the pile. If the card matches a card in his or her hand, the player lays down the pair.

d. Players continue taking turns and asking for cards until one player matches all of his or her cards. The player with the most matching pairs wins the game.

5. Answer any questions before students play independently. Then divide the class into pairs and have students play on their own. Circulate around the room to check that students are matching synonyms correctly and that they understand the rules of the game.

6. As a follow-up, extend the learning by having students write sentences using four of the words they "won." Then have students store their cards in an envelope and save them for a future game.

Variation of the Game

Have students create a list of antonyms and make word cards for a new version of the game.

Beat the Clock

Objective

Students will present examples of different parts of speech.

Learning parts of speech helps students see that words have particular functions. Use this game to reinforce students' understanding of different parts of speech. Play the game after your class is familiar with the terms *noun, verb, pronoun, adjective,* and *adverb.*

1. Ahead of time, make cardstock copies of the **Beat the Clock Challenge Cards reproducibles (pages 20–21)**. Cut out the game cards and place each set in a separate paper bag. Next, write these phrases on slips of paper: *noun that names an animal, verb that ends with **e**, adjective that describes a worm, adverb that starts with **b**.* Place the slips of paper in a third bag. Set aside the materials.

2. Help students prepare for the game by reviewing the parts of speech. Write the following sentence on the board: *The old man walked slowly.* Ask students to identify the noun in the sentence. *(man)* Then have them identify the verb *(walked)*, adjective *(old)*, and adverb *(slowly)*. Remind the class that these words illustrate different parts of speech.

3. Tell students that they will be playing a team game called Beat the Clock. Have four volunteers model the game as you explain how to play. Use the bag with the slips of paper for the demonstration.

   a. The first player draws a paper slip from the bag and reads it aloud.

   b. The player responds by naming a word that fits the description. For example, if the slip says *adverb that starts with **b***, a player might say *bravely* or *brightly*.

   c. The first player passes the bag to the next player who draws a paper slip, reads it aloud, and responds.

   d. Repeat the steps with the remaining players.

Materials

- Beat the Clock Challenge Cards reproducibles
- cardstock
- scissors
- 3 paper bags
- slips of paper
- clock or watch with second hand

978-1-4129-5930-8

4. Tell the class that they will play the game as two teams, and the goal is to collect as many game cards as possible in one minute. Explain the rules of the game:
    - Anyone on the team may give a response as soon as a card is read. Teams collect a game card for each correct response. You will determine if the response is correct.
    - If no one can give a response, the card is returned to the bag and a new card is drawn.
    - No word can be used more than once as a response. (For example, if *peanut* was used as *noun that begins with **p***, then it cannot be used again as *noun that is a compound word.*)
    - The team with the most cards wins the game.

5. Answer any questions, and then divide the class into two teams. Have each team gather in a different area of the room. Give a paper bag with game cards to the first team, and invite the other team to watch. At the end of a minute, stop the game and give the second paper bag to the other team for a new game.

6. As a follow-up, have students discuss the categories on the game cards. Ask: *Did you have difficulty thinking of examples for any of the categories? Which were the easiest? Which were the most difficult?*

Extended Learning

Discuss with students other kinds of phrases that could be used on the game cards, such as *noun that has two syllables* or *verb that has **oo***. List their suggestions on the board. Then have students help you make game cards for a new round of games.

Beat the Clock Challenge Cards

verb that tells how an animal moves	adjective that describes your school	pronoun that is plural
noun that tells what you might see at night	adverb that describes how a person might walk	adverb that describes how a person might talk
verb that tells what a frog does	noun that begins with **p**	verb that begins with **s**
adjective that describes a bear	adjective that describes water	adverb that ends in **ly**
noun that ends in **l**	verb that tells what you do at home	noun that is a compound word
verb that begins with **h**	noun that ends in **n**	adjective that begins with **b**

Beat the Clock Challenge Cards

verb that tells how a person moves	noun that tells what you see at school	verb that tells what a snake does
pronoun that is not a plural	noun that ends in **d**	verb that begins with **m**
adjective that describes an insect	adverb that describes where something happens	noun that begins with **l**
adjective that describes sand	verb that tells what you can do in water	noun that ends in **g**
noun that is plural	adverb that describes how something happens	verb that begins with **l**
adverb that begins with **s**	adjective that describes a vegetable	adjective that begins with **t**

Literature Hop

Materials
- Literature Hop Game Board reproducible
- Literature Hop Game Cards reproducible
- cardstock
- resealable plastic bags or manila envelopes
- counters or other game markers
- class literature books

Objective
Students will review a story by answering questions about its content and structure.

Literature studies help students analyze the structure and development of a story as well as foster their appreciation for books. This game provides a fun alternative to traditional literature lessons and class discussions. Have students play the game after the class has completed reading a core literature book.

1. Ahead of time, copy the **Literature Hop Game Board** and **Literature Hop Game Cards reproducibles (pages 24–25)** on cardstock. Copy one game board and one set of cards for every two students. Laminate the game boards and cards for durability if you wish. Store the game sets in resealable plastic bags or manila envelopes.

2. Prepare the class for the game by displaying a literature book they are studying and asking two or three questions to review the story. For example: *What was the story about? Who was the main character? What was the character's problem?*

3. Tell students that they will continue reviewing the book with a partner. Explain that instead of discussing the story, they will be playing a board game. Then divide the class into pairs, and give each pair a game board, a set of game cards, and two counters for markers. Have students keep a copy of the literature book as a reference during the game.

4. Explain and model the rules of the game.
   a. Players shuffle the game cards and place them facedown in a pile.
   b. Players take turns drawing a card, giving a response, and moving their game marker on the game board the appropriate number of spaces.
   c. The player who reaches the end of the game board first wins the game.

5. Read aloud several game cards, and invite volunteers to respond. Explain that some cards have questions with only one correct answer (e.g., *Name the author of the book*), while other questions have a variety of possible answers (e.g., *Name one word that describes the main character*). Tell students that they can refer to the book any time they wish. Answer any questions, and then invite students to play independently.

6. Circulate around the room and monitor students' responses to check their understanding of the game rules and their comprehension of the book. Help students read the game cards as needed.

7. As a follow-up, ask questions that allow students to share some of the responses they gave in the game. Ask questions such as: *What word did you use to describe the book? What did you think was the most exciting part of the book? Which character did you say you would like to play if the book was made into a movie?*

Literature Hop Game Board

Start

You lost a library book. LOSE A TURN

You read the end of the book first. GO BACK 2 SPACES

Finish

978-1-4129-5930-8 • © Corwin Press

Literature Hop Game Cards

Say the theme of the story. Move 2 spaces and take another turn.	Would you like the main character as a friend? Explain. Move 2 spaces.	Describe one main event and why it was important. Move 2 spaces.
Tell which character you would play if the book were a movie. Move 1 space.	Tell why the story was or was not interesting. Move 1 space.	State a question you would ask the author. Move 1 space.
Say one word to describe the main character. Move 2 spaces.	Describe the book's setting. Move 2 spaces.	Describe the problem and how it was solved. Move 2 spaces and take another turn.
Name the book title. Move 1 space.	Name the book's author. Move 1 space.	Name the book's main character. Move 1 space.

Summarize the book in four sentences or less. Move 2 spaces.

Say one word that describes the book. Move 1 space.

Describe the most exciting part of the book. Move 2 spaces.

Name a side character. Move 1 space.

Knowledge Quest

Materials
- 5 copies of a nonfiction book
- chart paper
- markers
- 5 large rubber bands
- clock or watch

Objectives
Students will make predictions about a book based on its cover. Students will scan the book to check their predictions.

Making predictions is an important critical thinking skill. It requires students to use given pieces of information to make reasonable assumptions. In this game, students study the cover of a nonfiction book and predict the type of content they will find inside.

1. Show your class a nonfiction book and read aloud the title. Tell the class that the cover of a book can help readers predict what they will find inside. Then discuss the following questions to guide students into thinking about the book's content:
   - *What does the picture on the cover show?*
   - *What is the topic of the book?*
   - *Do you think the book was written to entertain or to give facts?*
   - *What is one question that might be answered in the book?*

2. Tell students that they will be working in teams to predict what kinds of questions they think the book will answer. Add that they will earn one point for every question whose answer is found in the book. Then divide the class into five teams. Give each team a copy of the nonfiction book, a sheet of chart paper, a marker, and a rubber band. Have students wrap the rubber band around the book to keep it from opening.

978-1-4129-5930-8

3. Explain and model the rules of the game.
    a. When you say *go*, team members start sharing ideas with one another. Teams write their questions on the chart paper.
    b. After 15 minutes, say *stop*. Teams remove the rubber band from their book and skim through the pages.
    c. If students find the answers to any of their questions, they check off the question on their chart and then fill in the answer.
    d. Teams earn one point for each question they checked off and answered. The team with the most points wins the game.

4. Model writing questions about a book. For example, for a book titled *Journey to the Planets*, write questions such as: *Who was the first astronaut in space? Has anyone taken pictures from outer space?* Invite volunteers to suggest other questions. Answer any questions and then begin the game.

5. Circulate among the teams to check that students are writing appropriate questions. If they need help, guide them by asking questions such as the following:
    • *What does the title on the cover make you think of?*
    • *What kinds of things would you want to know if you were reading about this topic?*
    • *If you were writing a book with this title, what would you put in the book?*

6. After the game, post students' charts at the front of the room so students can compare and learn from the questions they created.

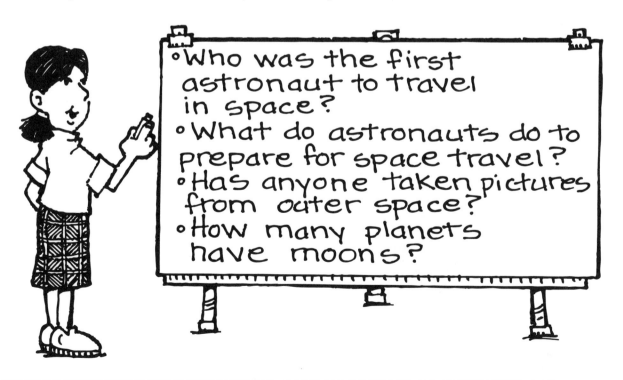

CHAPTER 2

Mathematics

Fraction Match

Objective

Students will match problem cards displaying addition and subtraction of like fractions with answer cards displaying sums and differences.

Materials
- Fraction Match Cards reproducible
- cardstock
- scissors

In third grade, students begin simple operations with fractions. The following game reinforces addition and subtraction skills with like fractions (fractions that have the same denominators). Invite students to play the game after they already have had some experience adding and subtracting like fractions. Students should also be familiar with the terms *numerator* and *denominator*.

1. Ahead of time, copy the **Fraction Match Cards reproducible (page 30)** onto cardstock for each student.

2. Prepare students for the game by drawing a circle on the board, dividing it into fourths, and shading one fourth. Ask the class to state what part is shaded. *(1/4)* Write *1/4* on the board. Then shade two more fourths in a different color. Ask how many fourths are shaded now. *(3/4)* Write *1/4 + 2/4 = 3/4* on the board.

3. Remind the class that the bottom number of a fraction is the *denominator*; it describes *what kind of parts* students are working with. Point out that the top number is the *numerator*; it shows *how many parts* students are working with.

4. Review with students that when like fractions are added, the numerators are added but the denominators remain the same. Explain that this is because the kinds of parts (in the example, fourths) remain the same.

5. Draw a rectangle on the board, divide it into eighths, and shade five eighths. Ask the class to state what part is shaded. Write the answer on the board in fraction form. *(5/8)* Next, cross out four of the shaded parts. Ask how many eighths are shaded now. *(1/8)* Write *5/8 − 4/8 = 1/8* on the board. Tell the class that when subtracting like fractions, the numerators are subtracted but the denominators remain the same.

6. Tell students that they will be playing a memory game to practice adding and subtracting fractions. Then divide the class into pairs, and give each pair two copies of the Fraction Match Cards reproducible.

7. Point out that the reproducible is divided into 16 cards. Read the problem on the first card (*1/3 + 1/3 =*), and call on a student to state the answer. (*2/3*) Point out that there is an answer to the right of each problem on the page. Instruct students to write *Answers* at the top of the page. They will be keeping the page as a reference for the game.

8. Direct partners to cut out the cards on their second copy of the reproducible. Have students shuffle the cards and arrange them facedown in a 4 x 4 grid. Then explain and model the rules of the game.

   a. Players pick up two cards at a time. They check to see if the problem and answer cards match.
   b. If the cards match, the player keeps the cards and takes another turn. If they do not match, the player returns the cards to their original positions and his or her partner takes a turn.
   c. Players may draw pictures on scrap paper or refer to their Answers page to help them answer any problems.
   d. The game ends when all of the cards have been matched. The player with the most matches wins!

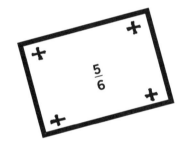

9. Pick up two cards. Read them aloud and ask a volunteer if they make a match. Repeat this several times and then begin the game. Circulate during the game to check that students understand the rules and are able to match the cards correctly. Remind students that part of the challenge is remembering where they have seen cards before so they can find them to make matches later.

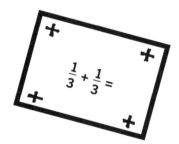

10. As a follow-up, discuss the following questions to evaluate learning: *When adding and subtracting like fractions, why don't the denominators change? How is adding and subtracting like fractions similar to adding and subtracting whole numbers?* Invite students to help you make additional game cards to use in future games of Fraction Match.

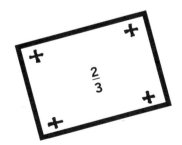

Name _____ Date _____

Fraction Match Cards

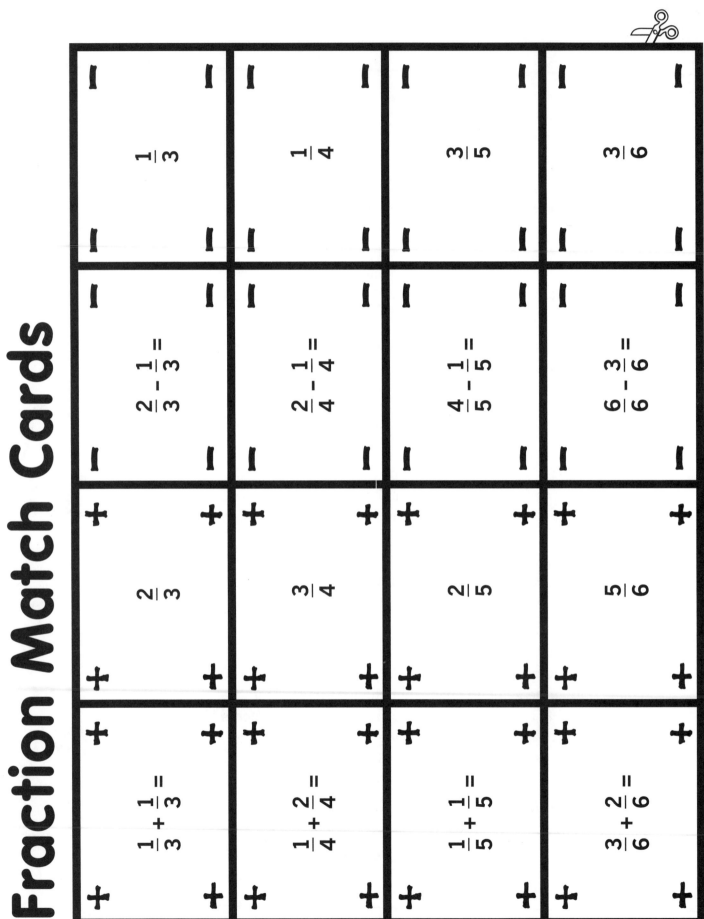

$\dfrac{1}{3}$	$\dfrac{1}{4}$	$\dfrac{3}{5}$	$\dfrac{3}{6}$
$\dfrac{2}{3} - \dfrac{1}{3} =$	$\dfrac{2}{4} - \dfrac{1}{4} =$	$\dfrac{4}{5} - \dfrac{1}{5} =$	$\dfrac{6}{6} - \dfrac{3}{6} =$
$\dfrac{2}{3}$	$\dfrac{3}{4}$	$\dfrac{2}{5}$	$\dfrac{5}{6}$
$\dfrac{1}{3} + \dfrac{1}{3} =$	$\dfrac{1}{4} + \dfrac{2}{4} =$	$\dfrac{1}{5} + \dfrac{1}{5} =$	$\dfrac{3}{6} + \dfrac{2}{6} =$

Reproducible

978-1-4129-5930-8 • © Corwin Press

Switch!

Objective

Students will identify factors of given numbers.

Materials
• none

The ability to quickly recognize factors and products is a skill that third graders must develop in order to successfully tackle multiplication and division problems. It is also a prerequisite for understanding upper-grade math concepts such as the greatest common factor, the least common multiple, and common denominators. This game provides students with practice in identifying factors of a given number. Play the game after students have had experience working with multiplication and division facts.

1. Write ____ × ____ = 12 on the board. Ask a student to fill in the blanks with two numbers. Then write ____ × ____ = 12 again, and ask a second student to write two different numbers. Repeat one more time until the numbers *3, 4, 6, 2, 12,* and *1* have been written. Tell students that these numbers are *factors* of 12. Explain that factors are numbers that are multiplied together to get a *product.* The numbers *3, 4, 6, 2, 12,* and *1* are factors of 12 because they can each be multiplied to produce 12. Put another way, a factor is a number that divides evenly into a given number.

2. Write *20* on the board. Have the class determine the factors of 20 by calling on students to write multiplication facts for 20 on the board. *(4 × 5, 2 × 10, 20 × 1)* Ask students to identify the factors of 20. *(4, 5, 2, 10, 20, 1)*

3. Next, tell them that you are going to say some numbers. Have students raise their hand when they hear a number that is a factor of 20. Then slowly say: *3, 6, 11, 12, 5.* When you say 5, check that students raise their hands. Help students see that they can determine if 5 is a factor of 20 by asking themselves: *Does 5 times a number equal 20?* They might also ask: *Can 20 be divided evenly by 5?*

4. Continue by saying: *7, 2, 15, 13, 4, 9, 1, 8, 10, 20,* and check that students raise their hands for *1, 2, 4, 10,* and *20.*

5. Tell students that they are going to play a game in which they must listen for factors. Explain and model the rules of the game.

   a. Write a number (e.g., *36*) on the board. Then slowly say a list of numbers (e.g., *10, 5, 13, 7, 9*).

   b. When players hear a number that is a factor of the number on the board (e.g., *9*), they jump out of their seats. Say: *Yes—9 is a factor of 36!*

   c. Players now rush to switch places with a classmate. Players can change seats with anyone in the room as long as they are seated when you start calling numbers again. (For an extra challenge, allow students limited time to find a new seat. If they aren't seated on time, they are out of the game.)

   d. When everyone is seated, ask: *What times 9 is 36?* Call on a student to give the answer. *(4)*

   e. The game continues with you naming more numbers (e.g., *8, 15, 11, 6*) and players listening for any number that is a factor of the number on the board.

   f. Begin a new game by writing a new number on the board.

6. Write a number on the board, and invite the class to play a practice round. Once students have a good understanding of how to play, begin a real game.

7. After the game, discuss the following questions:
   • *How does knowing multiplication and division help you play the game?*
   • *What can you do when you are trying to figure out if a number is a factor?*

978-1-4129-5930-8

Remainder Cross-Out

Objective

Students will divide two-digit numbers by one-digit divisors. They will then check the numbers on a grid to see if they match the remainders in their quotients.

Third graders are just starting to explore the concept of long division. Reinforce their division skills by combining division practice with an engaging strategy game.

1. Ahead of time, photocopy and cut out one spinner from the **Spinner Pattern reproducible (page 35)** for every four students.

2. Set out 23 pencils and ten paper bags. Ask the class how many bags would be filled if you placed three pencils in each bag. Then call on a student to demonstrate. (There will be seven bags filled, with two pencils leftover.) Write $23 \div 3 = 7\ R2$ on the board. Point to the numbers in the division sentence as you point out that 23 shows the number being divided, 3 shows how many are in each group, 7 shows the number of equal groups, and 2 shows the remainder—the number leftover.

3. Distribute drawing paper to students. Write $19 \div 4$ on the board, and have students draw "sticks" and circle them in groups to solve the problem. (Four groups of four sticks should be circled, with three leftover.) Write $19 \div 4 = 4\ R3$ on the board. Next, have students solve $39 \div 3$. Students will discover that this problem results in 13 equal groups and no remainder (or a remainder of 0).

4. Tell students that they will continue practicing division by playing a game called Remainder Cross-Out. Then divide the class into groups of four, and give each group a spinner, a pencil, a paper clip, and several sheets of drawing paper. Show students how to place a paper clip over the center of the spinner and place the tip of the pencil through the end of the paper clip. Students will flick the paper clip "arrow" in order to spin for numbers during the game.

5. Have two volunteers demonstrate how to play the game as you explain the rules. Ask the students to draw their game boards on the board so the whole class can see them.
   a. Each player draws a 3 x 3 grid and then writes the numbers 0–8 in it. The numbers stand for remainders. Any number may be used up to three times. Players may decide not to use some numbers at all.

b. The first player spins the spinner three times and uses the numbers to make a division problem—the first two numbers form the two-digit dividend and the third is the divisor (e.g., the numbers 4, 8, and 5 would generate 48 ÷ 5).

c. Players work together to draw pictures or use another strategy (such as a knowledge of multiplication facts) to solve the division problem and then write the answer next to the grid.

d. If the answer has a remainder (e.g., 48 ÷ 5 has a remainder of 3), both players check to see if the number appears on their grid. If it does, they cross it off. (If the remainder is 3 and there are two 3s on a grid, players only cross off one 3 for this turn.)

e. Then the second player uses the spinner to create a division problem. Both students work together to solve the problem and then check their grids for the remainder.

f. The first player to cross off all the numbers in his or her grid wins the game.

6. Spin the spinner three times, and write the three numbers on the board. Have volunteers help you write and solve the division problem. Ask the class to identify the remainder and the number they would cross off on the grid. Answer any questions, and then have students play independently.

7. After the game, have students discuss the following questions:
   - *Were some remainders more common than others?*
   - *Why couldn't the number 9 be used as a remainder on the grid?*
   - *What strategies did you use to solve the division problems?*
   - *If you played again, how would you select the numbers for your grid?*

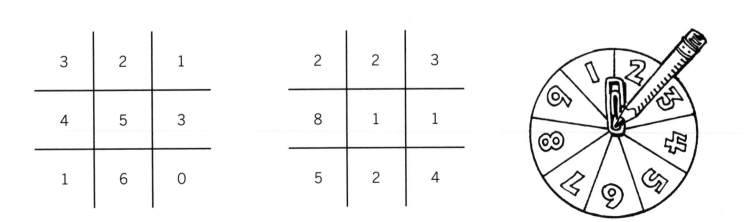

978-1-4129-5930-8

Spinner Pattern

What's the Rule?

Materials
- What's the Rule? reproducible
- cardstock
- picture of a bike
- scissors
- counters or drawing paper

Objective
Students will analyze function tables and determine the rules that generated the results.

Students can develop an understanding of number relationships by analyzing and creating number patterns. In this game, students study function tables to determine the "rules" used to generate the numbers.

1. Ahead of time, make a cardstock copy of the **What's the Rule? reproducible (page 38)** for every two students.

2. Display a picture of a bike, and ask the class how many wheels it has. *(2)* Ask how many wheels two bikes would have. *(4)* Then ask how many wheels five bikes would have. *(10)* Discuss how students got each answer.

3. Tell students that they can use a table to show the relationship between the number of bikes and the number of wheels. Draw on the board a table similar to the ones shown on the reproducible. Write *1* in the Input column. Tell the class that this number stands for the number of bikes. Next, write *2* in the Output column. Tell the class that this number stands for the number of wheels on one bike. Repeat the activity for two bikes and for five bikes. Help students see that given the number of bikes, the rule for determining the number of wheels is "multiply by 2."

4. Draw another table on the board. This time, tell students that you will start with the number of wheels on a tricycle. Then write *3* in the Input column. Ask how many tricycles there would be if there were three wheels. Write *1* in the Output column. Next, write *9* in the Input column. Ask a student to write the corresponding number of tricycles. *(3)* Repeat with 12 wheels and 18 wheels. *(4, 6)* Ask students to state the rule for determining how many tricycles there are when given the number of wheels. *(divide by 3)*

5. Tell students that they are going to work in pairs to make tables like those on the board. Then divide the class into pairs, and give each pair a copy of the reproducible.
   a. Ask each pair to think of four math rules, such as "add 5," "subtract 10," "multiply by 4," or "divide by 6."
   b. Direct them to use the rules to generate numbers for each table on the reproducible. For example, if the rule is "add 5," they could write *3* in the Input column and *8* in the Output column.

 978-1-4129-5930-8

c. As students work, tell them not to share their tables with the rest of the class because you will be using the tables in a special relay game. Have students use counters or draw pictures to help them determine each output.

6. Circulate around the room to check that students complete their tables correctly.

7. Have students cut out the cards along the solid lines to make four game cards. Instruct partners to write their names and the corresponding rules on the backs of the cards.

8. Collect the cards, shuffle them, and lay them faceup in a pile. Tell students that they will be playing a relay game to help them practice recognizing number rules. Then divide the class into two teams, and send the teams to the back of the room. Explain and model the rules of the game.
   a. One player from each team comes to the front of the room. Flash a card with one of the function tables.
   b. Players study the card to see how the numbers in the first column relate to those in the second column. The first player to state the correct number rule gets to keep the card for his or her team.
   c. Players run back to their teams, and the next two players advance. The game continues until everyone has had a turn or until all the cards have been played. The team with the most cards wins the game.

9. Play a practice round to make sure students understand how to play. Then begin a real game.

10. As a follow-up, ask students to share the strategies they used to determine the rule for each card.

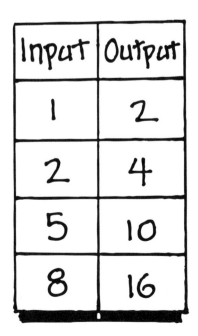

Input	Output
1	2
2	4
5	10
8	16

Name _____   Date _____

What's the Rule?

What's the Rule?

Input	Output

What's the Rule?

Input	Output

What's the Rule?

Input	Output

What's the Rule?

Input	Output

Polygon String Shapes

Objective

Students will form geometric shapes to match given criteria.

Materials
• string
• scissors

Geometry involves working with a variety of figures and understanding how these figures are distinct and unique. The following game not only helps develop students' ability to distinguish polygons, it also encourages critical thinking and promotes cooperative learning.

1. Ahead of time, cut string into 20-foot-long pieces. Cut one piece for every group of five or six students.

2. Review the definition of a *polygon* (a closed, flat shape that is made up of three or more line segments) with the class. Then call on a student to draw a polygon on the board. Ask the class to name the polygon and state any distinguishing features. For example, if the student draws a rectangle, point out that the figure has four sides, four corners, four right angles, and two equal sides. Repeat the activity by calling on a second student to draw a different shape.

3. Tell students that they will be working in groups to form polygon shapes. Next, take the class outdoors to a large, open area. Divide the class into groups of five or six students, and give each group a 20-foot length of string.

4. Tell students that they will be making shapes with string. Then have one group demonstrate. Direct the group to make a shape with three sides and three corners. Have three students act as the corners and hold the string taut between them. Let students who are not needed for the corners stand inside the group's completed shape, or let them stand between two students and hold the string to help form a side.

5. After the demonstration, have groups spread out so that they have room to form their shapes. Then explain and model how to play the game.

    a. Call out the instructions for a shape.

    b. Give groups one minute to form each shape. Students should take turns acting as the corners of the shapes.

    c. Circulate among the groups to make sure they are forming the shapes correctly and cooperatively.

6. Answer any questions, and then begin the game. Give directions such as the following:

- *Make a shape with four sides and four angles.*
- *Make a triangle with three equal sides.*
- *Make a triangle with no equal sides.*
- *Make a parallelogram.*
- *Make a shape that has as at least five sides.*
- *Make a shape that has exactly one pair of parallel sides.*
- *Make a shape that has at least one right angle.*

7. Ask the groups to compare their shapes. Ask how the shapes are similar and how they are different. To make a parallelogram, for example, one group might form a shape with no right angles, while another might form a rectangle or a square.

8. After the game, discuss the following questions:

- *For which instructions did everyone have to make the same shape?* (An equilateral triangle is the only "triangle with three equal sides." All equilateral triangles have the same shape, but they can vary in size.)
- *Which instructions resulted in two or more different shapes?* (Responses will vary. Any quadrilateral, such as a square, rectangle, parallelogram, or trapezoid, would satisfy the criteria for "a shape with four sides and four angles.")

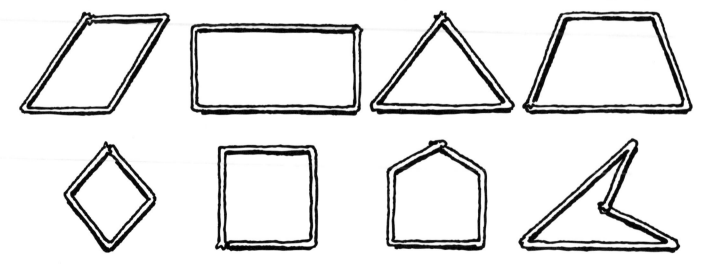

978-1-4129-5930-8

Symmetry Scavenger Hunt

Objective

Students will look for pictures of symmetrical objects and determine how many lines of symmetry each figure has.

Materials
- 9" x 12" construction paper
- 12" x 18" construction paper
- 9" paper square
- scissors
- magazine pictures of symmetrical shapes (e.g., vase, lamp, table)
- magazines
- glue

Symmetry appears all around us—in nature, in works of art, and in common human-made items. Use this game to develop students' understanding of symmetry and help them become more aware of symmetrical objects in their world.

1. Get students thinking about symmetry. Hold up a 9" x 12" sheet of construction paper, and have students name its shape. *(rectangle)* Fold the paper in half lengthwise, and then unfold it to reveal the two halves. Point out that the halves match exactly. Explain that when a shape can be folded to make two matching halves, it is said to have *symmetry*. Then point to the fold line. Explain that the line that divides a symmetrical shape in half is called the *line of symmetry*.

2. Holding the same paper, ask the class if it can be folded in half another way. Call on a student to demonstrate. (The student should fold the paper in half crosswise.) Tell the class that because a rectangle can be folded in half in two different ways, it has two lines of symmetry.

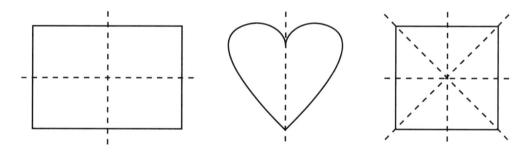

3. Fold another 9" x 12" sheet of construction paper in half and cut out a heart shape. Ask how many lines of symmetry the new figure has. *(one)* Next, hold up a 9" paper square, and ask students to predict how many lines of symmetry it has. Then fold the paper in half lengthwise, crosswise, and diagonally to show that a square has four lines of symmetry.

4. Tell students that they will be playing Symmetry Scavenger Hunt, a game in which they earn points for every symmetrical shape they find. Explain that the goal is to collect as many points as possible. Then divide the class into pairs, and give each pair a 12" x 18" sheet of construction paper.

5. Show students two or three magazine pictures of symmetrical shapes. Discuss the number of lines of symmetry for each shape. Then explain and model the rules of the game.

   a. Partners cut out examples of symmetrical objects and glue them onto construction paper to make a collage.

   b. Partners must find a variety of shapes to earn points. The pair with the most points wins the game.

6. Write the following scoring information on the board to guide students as they play:

   • Squares, rectangles, circles: one point each
   • Symmetrical shapes with exactly one line of symmetry: two points each
   • Symmetrical shapes (not a square, rectangle, or circle) with two or more lines of symmetry: three points each

7. Display the magazine pictures from Step 5, and ask students how many points they would earn for each shape. Answer any questions, and then begin the game.

8. As students work on their collages, ask questions to check their understanding of symmetry: *How many lines of symmetry does this figure have? Where is the line of symmetry for this figure? Do you see symmetrical objects in the classroom?*

9. After the game, display the collages on a bulletin board. Invite students to choose an object and identify the number of lines of symmetry.

978-1-4129-5930-8

Estimation Station Relay

Objective

Students will fill a container with water, estimate the volume, and then check their estimate by measuring.

Materials
- 1-cup liquid measuring cup
- three 2-liter soda bottles labeled *1, 2, 3*
- three 3-ounce paper cups
- three 1-gallon pails

Students need hands-on experiences measuring a variety of items in order to grasp what measurement is all about. They also need opportunities to estimate measurements before they actually check them. The following relay race provides a fun way for students to practice measuring volume.

1. Set out a liquid measuring cup, and ask the class what it is used to measure. *(the amount of liquid in a container)* Invite students to tell you how much liquid they think the measuring cup holds. Then tell them that they will be practicing their measuring skills by playing a relay game.

2. Take the class outdoors to a large, open area. Bring along three soda bottles, three paper cups, and three large pails.

3. Divide the class into three teams. Fill the pails with water, and have the teams line up behind them. Give the first player on each team a paper cup. Set a soda bottle about 20 yards away from each team.

4. Ask one of the students who is holding a cup to demonstrate the relay while you explain the game.
   a. The first player on each team uses the cup to scoop water from the pail.
   b. Players run to their team's soda bottle and pour the water from the cup into the bottle.
   c. Players then run back to their team and hand the cup to the next player.
   d. The game ends when each team member has poured a cup of water into the bottle two times. The team with the highest level of water wins the relay.

5. Answer any questions, and then begin the relay. After several minutes, stop the game and have students compare the level of the water in all the soda bottles.

6. After the game, empty the pails of water, but keep the water in the soda bottles. Bring all the items back to the classroom.

7. Display the soda bottles in front of the class. Ask students to estimate how much water the bottles contain. Have them write their estimate for each bottle on a sheet of paper.

8. Ask students to suggest ways to measure the water. Help them discover that they can measure the water in each bottle separately. Explain that they can use the measuring cup to pour out one cup of water at a time and keep track of how many cups are filled.

9. Call on students to help you pour out the water from the bottles. Write the measurement for each bottle on the board. Afterward, have students check their papers to see who had the most accurate estimates.

978-1-4129-5930-8

Unlucky Royals

Objective

Students will play a card game in which they must determine how to attain the greatest chance of scoring points and winning.

Materials
• 6 decks of playing cards

Games of probability and chance are great fun for students. They also provide opportunities for predicting and evaluating outcomes. This card game requires students to analyze the game situation and maximize their chances of winning.

1. Show the class a deck of playing cards. Ask students to name some card games they have played and to describe the strategies that helped them win. For example, Crazy Eights is a game in which players get rid of cards by laying down cards of a particular suit; laying down an eight allows a player to change the suit being played. Students might say that they hold on to their eights until they really need to use them.

2. Tell students that they will be playing a card game in which they earn points by picking up as many cards as possible during their turn. Explain that number cards are worth their face value and aces are worth one.

3. Demonstrate how to play the game as you explain the rules.
   a. Draw a card from the pile and write its value on the board. Pick up another card and do the same. Discuss the number of points earned. (For example, if you pick up a four and a ten, you would earn 14 points.)
   b. A player can pick up as many cards as he or she wants during a turn. However, if the player picks up a "royal card"— a king, jack, or queen—he or she loses all the cards won in that turn. Those cards are set aside and not played again.
   c. When a player stops picking up cards or when he or she is forced to stop because of an unlucky royal card, the player to the left takes a turn. (If the first card a player picks up is a royal card, the player simply misses his or her turn.)

d. The game ends when all the cards have been picked up. The player with the most points wins.

4. Have students tally your score as you draw cards. Make sure they know what to do when you draw a royal card.

5. Divide the class into six groups, and give each group a deck of playing cards and writing paper. Have a dealer in each group shuffle the cards and place them facedown in a pile. Then invite students to play the game.

6. Provide ample time for all the groups to finish playing at least two rounds. As students play, encourage them to think of strategies for retaining their points.

7. As a follow-up, ask students to share their strategies for winning. Ask the following questions to help guide their thinking:
   - *How did you decide whether or not to stop picking up cards?* (For example, did students always stop after only one or two cards, or did they make a decision based on how many royal cards had already been picked up?)
   - *How many royal cards are in a deck?* (12) *How would the game be affected if the jacks were taken out of the deck?* (There would be less chance of drawing a royal card.)
   - *Suppose only the kings were the "unlucky" cards. How would this affect your playing strategy?* (When only four cards out of 52 are unlucky, there is less likelihood of picking up an unlucky card. There is a higher probability of picking up more cards without losing them.)

CHAPTER 3

Science

Tag the Target

Objective

Students will make a simple lever and use it to fling an object onto a target.

Materials
- stapler
- six 12-inch rulers
- 6 rectangular toy blocks
- 6 socks
- six 12" x 18" sheets of construction paper
- masking tape

Machines are designed to make work easier. All machines work on the same principle—they move things when force is applied. Use this game to give students an opportunity to make a lever and observe how it works.

1. Call on a student to hold a stapler. Point out the weight of the stapler. Next, make a simple lever by putting a small block on your desk and resting a ruler on the block. Put the stapler on the end of the ruler that is closest to the block. Have the student press down the other end of the ruler. The student will discover that he or she can lift the stapler easily. Tell the class that the ruler and block form a simple machine called a *lever*. People use levers to lift weight with little effort.

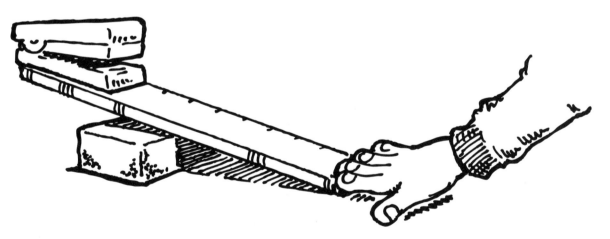

2. Tell students that they will be playing a game that lets them experiment with levers. Divide the class into six teams. Give each team a ruler, a toy block, a rolled-up sock, and a sheet of construction paper.

3. Show students how they can make a lever by placing the block on the floor and resting the ruler on top of it. Instruct students to tape down their sheet of construction paper one or two feet away from their lever.

4. Explain and model how to play the game.
    a. Team members take turns putting the sock on one end of the ruler and pushing down on the other end to toss the sock into the air.
    b. The team scores one point each time the sock lands on the paper. Teams keep track of their score on paper. The team with the most points wins.

5. Have several volunteers use their levers to hurl a sock through the air. Then allow teams time to practice with their sock and lever before they begin the game.

6. Circulate around the room, and encourage teams to experiment with the position of their block and ruler to make their sock land on the target.

7. After the game, discuss the results with the class. Let students share how they adjusted their levers to get the desired effects. Guide them to see that moving the block nearer or farther away from the sock affected how high and how far the sock was tossed.

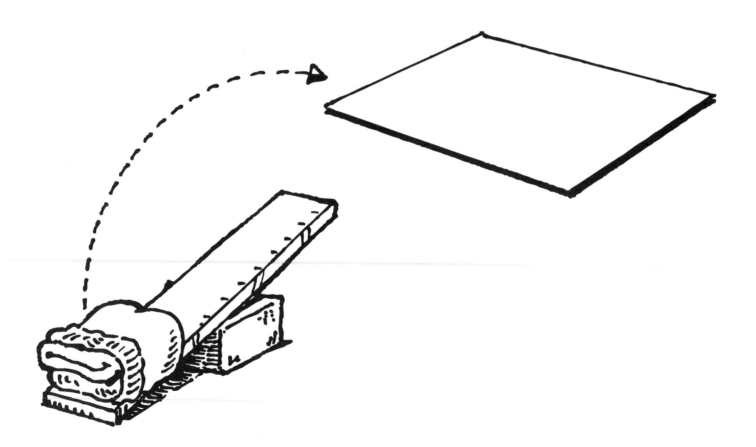

978-1-4129-5930-8

Pass the Potato

Objective

Students will display an understanding of the different forms of energy and give examples of each.

Materials
- flashlight
- chart paper
- beanbag
- music recording
- CD or cassette player

Energy is the ability to do work or to cause change. Energy makes it possible for living things to grow and reproduce. It results in movements like a ball bouncing or a kite flying. In this fast-paced game, students review energy and its different forms. Play the game as a culmination of your students' study of energy.

1. Darken the room and turn on a flashlight. Ask students what form of energy is being illustrated. Help the class see that the flashlight shows light energy at work. Also help students see that the battery inside the flashlight is an example of stored energy. The energy stored inside the battery gets used whenever the flashlight is turned on.

2. Review the different forms of energy and list them on a chart. (Adjust the list to reflect the terminology used in your previous lessons on energy.)

3. Have students give examples of each form of energy. (Some examples may illustrate more than one form of energy.) Add their ideas to the chart. Post the chart as a reference for the game. Following are some suggestions:
   - light energy—sun, lamp, candle, car headlights, flashlight
   - sound energy—musical instrument, someone shouting, door slamming, radio playing
   - electric energy—electric fan, television, computer, blender
   - heat energy—hot soup, heater, campfire, iron
   - stored energy—battery waiting to be used; food stored in people, animals, and plants; gasoline in the tank of a car

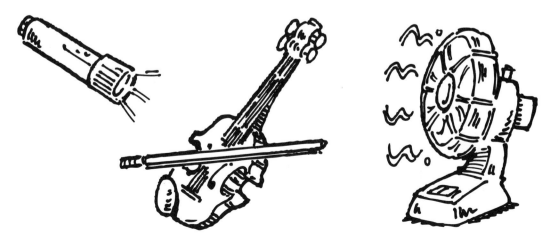

4. Tell students to sit or stand in a large circle for a game called Pass the Potato. Hold up a beanbag, and tell the class to pretend that it is a very hot potato. Explain and model the rules of the game.
   a. Players quickly pass the "potato" around the circle while the music plays.
   b. When the music stops, call out a form of energy, such as *light energy*. The player holding the beanbag must give a specific example of that energy form (e.g., *streetlight*).
   c. Players may refer to the chart if they need help with naming an example.
   d. Players continue passing the beanbag when the music starts and naming examples of energy when the music stops.

5. Play a practice round. Watch as the class passes the beanbag around to check that students understand the game. Then begin a real game.

6. After the game, discuss the following questions with the class to evaluate learning: *What forms of energy do you use at home? What would the world be like if there were no energy?*

Variation of the Game

If your students feel comfortable with increased competition, have those who cannot answer within five seconds leave the circle and sit down. Allow students to keep playing until there is only one student left.

978-1-4129-5930-8

Critter Categories

Objective

Students will recognize the traits of various animal groups and identify members of each group.

An important biology concept is that animals can be classified according to the physical traits that they share. A dog, a cat, and a bear, for example, look distinctly different, yet they are all classified as mammals. In the following game, students review different animal classifications and the traits that distinguish each group. Play the game after your class is familiar with the terms *mammal*, *bird*, *reptile*, *amphibian*, and *fish*.

1. Ahead of time, write a letter of the alphabet on each of 26 paper squares. Place the squares inside a paper bag. Set the bag aside.

2. Post pictures of three mammals on the board. Ask how the animals are alike, and guide the class to see that they are all mammals. Review the traits of mammals: they have fur or hair; they breathe with lungs; they give birth to live young; young drink their mother's milk; parents look after their babies for a period of time.

3. Display pictures of animals from other categories and review their traits.
   - Birds have feathers, two legs, and lungs; their young hatch from eggs.
   - Reptiles have dry, scaly skin; they breathe with lungs; most hatch from eggs.
   - Amphibians have thin, moist skin but no scales; young live in the water, while most adults live on land.
   - Fish live in water; they breathe with gills; most have scales.

4. Tell students that they will be playing a game called Critter Categories to help them think about the different animals that belong in various categories. Then give each student a copy of the **Critter Categories Game Sheet reproducible (page 53)**.

5. Guide students through a practice round of the game as you explain the rules.
   a. Set out the paper bag, and invite a student to draw a card.
   b. Write the letter on the board, and have students write it in the left column of their game sheet.
   c. At your signal, they fill in the first row by writing an animal name for each category. (For example, for the letter s, they might write *skunk* for a mammal, *swallow* for a bird, and so

Materials
- Critter Categories Game Sheet reproducible
- 26 three-inch paper squares
- paper lunch bag
- pictures of 3 distinct mammals (e.g., bear, deer, cat)
- pictures of birds, reptiles, amphibians, and fish
- clock or watch with minute hand (or stopwatch)

on.) Explain that both general names (such as *turtle*) and specific names (such as *green turtle*) may be used.

d. Say *go,* and give students one minute to complete a row. Then allow them to share their answers for each category.

e. Players score points as follows:

- An animal is listed by two or more students: one point.
- An animal is listed by only one student, but other animals have also been listed for the category (e.g., several students thought of mammals beginning with *s*, but only one wrote *seal*): two points for the unique animal.
- An animal is listed by only one student, and no other animals were listed for that category (e.g., only one student named an amphibian starting with *s*): three points for that animal.

6. Once students understand the rules and scoring, have them play a real game using the next row on their game sheet. Call on a student to draw a letter from the bag, and have the class write it in the second row of their game sheet. Then give students one minute to complete the row. Afterward, have students add up their points and write their score on the back of their paper. Repeat these steps until all the rows are filled.

7. Have students add up their scores for each row to get their final total. The student with the highest score wins.

8. As follow-up on a later date, let students work in groups to make posters of the different animal classifications. Have one group illustrate mammals, have another group illustrate birds, and so on. Allow students to refer to their game sheets for ideas.

978-1-4129-5930-8

Critter Categories Game Sheet

Directions: Write the chosen letter. At the signal, write an animal name for each column that begins with that letter. Repeat with a new letter.

Name _____ Date _____

Letter	Mammal	Bird	Reptile	Amphibian	Fish

Habitat Hunt

Materials
- index cards
- picture of the Arctic in winter

Objective

Students will identify different habitats and the animals they support.

Many different animals share the same habitat. Each animal has physical adaptations that help it survive in its environment. In this game, students match animals to their habitats. Play the game after students have been introduced to different types of habitats and the animals that live there.

1. Ahead of time, select four to six habitats and five animals per habitat. Write the name of each animal on an index card.

   Note: For four habitats and five animals each, you will need 20 students. For five habitats and five animals each, you will need 25 students. Adjust the game or the number of cards if the number of students in your class is not a multiple of five. For example, with 24 students, use four habitats and six animals each. With 23 students, use four habitats and six animals each, but count yourself as one of the players. With 22 students, use four habitats and six animals each, but place the two extra cards facedown in two separate places of the room; those cards can be assigned to "invisible" students A and B.

2. Show the class a picture of the Arctic in winter. Have students describe what they see. Tell the class that Arctic animals must be able to survive the region's freezing temperatures. Then write *Arctic* on the board, and have students name some Arctic animals (e.g., *Arctic fox, Arctic hare, caribou, lemming, musk ox, polar bear*). List the animals on the board beside the word *Arctic*.

3. Remind students that the place where an animal lives is called its *habitat,* and each habitat is home to a variety of animals. Then review other habitats, and have students give examples of animals that live in each one. Write suggestions on the board. Following are some examples:
   - African Savanna: elephant, gazelle, giraffe, lion, ostrich, zebra
   - Desert: coyote, dingo, iguana, rattlesnake, roadrunner, scorpion
   - Mountain: bighorn sheep, giant panda, mountain goat, pika, snow leopard, yak

- Ocean: dolphin, jellyfish, octopus, shark, tuna, whale
- Rainforest: gorilla, jaguar, sloth, spider monkey, tiger, tree frog
- Temperate Forest: bear, beaver, moose, otter, porcupine, squirrel

4. Tell students that they are going to review their knowledge of animal habitats by playing Habitat Hunt. Distribute writing paper and an animal card to each student. Have students keep their cards hidden. Ask them to write the habitat of their animal on the back of the card. (For example, a student who has a card reading *sloth* would write *rainforest* on the back.)

5. Explain and model the rules of the game.
   a. At your signal, players walk around the room and silently show their cards to one another.
   b. If players find a student whose animal shares the same habitat as theirs, they write that student's name and animal on a sheet of paper. Players should find four other animals besides the one on their card.
   c. The winner is the first player to find all four animals that share a habitat with his or her animal.

6. Invite several volunteers to the front of the room and demonstrate how to play. Ask questions to check students' understanding, and then begin the game.

7. As students move around the room, check that they can accurately spot an animal that shares the same habitat as their animal. If you observe that some students are unsure about the habitat of a particular animal, encourage them to refer to the list on the board.

8. When a student indicates that he or she has found four animals, check his or her paper. Let the rest of the class keep playing until all students have found the four animals that match the habitat listed on their card.

9. As a follow-up, have students share their findings so everyone can check that the animals and habitats were correctly matched. Invite students to think of other plants, animals, and characteristics of their habitats.

Rocky Challenge

Materials
- Rocky Challenge Game Cards reproducible
- cardstock
- scissors
- masking tape
- 3 or 4 different rocks

Objective
Students will review concepts learned during their study of rocks.

Rocks provide scientists with clues about the earth's history. Characteristics of rocks depend on how and where the rocks were formed. By studying rocks, scientists have been able to determine the structure of the earth and the forces that shape the planet. In this game, students review the concepts they learned from their study of rocks. If you wish, change the questions on the game cards to match the content of your curriculum.

1. Ahead of time, copy the **Rocky Challenge Game Cards reproducible (page 58)** onto cardstock. Cut out the cards, and tape them randomly in various places around the classroom.

2. Show students several rocks, and ask them to share what they have learned about rocks (e.g., *rocks are made of different minerals; rocks are used to make different things*).

3. Tell students that they will be playing a game to review the concepts they learned during their rock study. Then divide the class into pairs, and give each pair a sheet of writing paper. Instruct students to write the numbers *1–16* vertically down the left side of their paper.

4. Identify some of the cards displayed around the room. Point out that there are 16 question cards. Then explain and model the rules of the game.
   a. At your signal, partners walk around the room, read the questions on the cards, and write the answers on their paper.
   b. Partners may skip a question if they do not know the answer.
   c. Partners earn one point for each correct response.
   d. The first two pairs to finish and show you their papers earn three bonus points. The pair with the highest score wins the game.

5. Answer any questions students may have, and then invite them to begin at your signal. If students cannot find a card, give clues about its location (e.g., *Look to the right of the bookshelf*).

6. Inform the class when the first two pairs of students have finished writing their answers and have shown you their papers. Let the remaining students continue the game until everyone has found all 16 cards.

7. Have students check their answers with you (see the questions and answers below) and tally their points.

8. As a follow-up, have students create their own game cards for another game of Rocky Challenge.

Answers to Game Card Questions

1. What are rocks made of—clay, minerals, or cement? *(minerals)*

2. What is the outer layer of the earth called? *(crust)*

3. What is hot, liquid rock called? *(magma)*

4. What is a scientist who studies the earth called? *(geologist)*

5. Unscramble the letters. What is the name of this rock? tagrine *(granite)*

6. Which type of rock is formed from magma—igneous or sedimentary? *(igneous)*

7. True or False? Rocks are used for making jewelry. *(true)*

8. What will you *not* find at the earth's center—iron, gold, or nickel? *(gold)*

9. What are the three types of rock? *(igneous, sedimentary, metamorphic)*

10. Unscramble the letters. What is the name of this rock? tales *(slate)*

11. True or False? The earth is made up of five layers. *(false; it is made up of three layers)*

12. Which rock can float in water—pumice, sandstone, or marble? *(pumice)*

13. Which type of rock forms in layers—sedimentary or metamorphic? *(sedimentary)*

14. Which rock is formed from shells and bones— granite or limestone? *(limestone)*

15. What is the center of the earth called? *(core)*

16. True or False? One type of rock can change into another type. *(true)*

Rocky Challenge Game Cards

What are rocks made of—clay, minerals, or cement?	What is the outer layer of the earth called?	What is hot, liquid rock called?	What is a scientist who studies the earth called?
Unscramble the letters. What is the name of this rock? tagrine	Which type of rock is formed from magma—igneous or sedimentary?	True or False? Rocks are used for making jewelry.	What will you not find at the earth's center—iron, gold, or nickel?
What are the three types of rock?	Unscramble the letters. What is the name of this rock? tales	True or False? The earth is made up of five layers.	Which rock can float in water—pumice, sandstone, or marble?
Which type of rock forms in layers—sedimentary or metamorphic?	Which rock is formed from shells and bones—granite or limestone?	What is the center of the earth called?	True or False? One type of rock can change into another type.

       978-1-4129-5930-8 • © Corwin Press

Moon Jumps

Objective

Students will measure how high they can jump and then calculate the height of this jump on the moon.

The moon's gravity is six times weaker than that on Earth. In this game, students determine how the moon's gravity would affect their ability to jump.

Materials
- Moon Jumps reproducible
- pencil
- rolls of masking tape
- yardsticks or meter sticks
- 4 or 5 stepstools

1. Hold a pencil in front of you and then drop it. Tell students that the pencil falls because an invisible force called *gravity* pulls the pencil toward the center of the earth (the ground). Explain that there is gravity on the moon as well, but its force is only one-sixth of the gravity on Earth. A child weighing 60 pounds on Earth would weigh only 10 pounds on the moon because of the moon's weaker gravity.

2. Tell the class that gravity also affects how high a person can jump. A person would be able to jump six times higher on the moon than on Earth. Then tell students that they are going to play a game to see how high they could jump if they were on the moon.

3. Divide the class into teams of four or five students. Arrange the teams so that taller students (who may have an advantage) are spread out among the teams. Give each team a roll of masking tape, a yardstick, and a copy of the **Moon Jumps reproducible (page 61)**.

4. Call on a student to demonstrate the game as you explain how to play.
   a. The student holds a piece of masking tape and faces the wall. He or she jumps upward and places the tape on the wall as high as possible.
   b. Use a yardstick to measure the distance from the floor to the tape. (Students may need a stepstool to reach the tape.) Write the height on the board.
   c. The student then makes a second jump. Measure the second height and write it on the board.
   d. To get the average height of the two jumps, students must add the two measurements and then divide the sum by two. Use the sample jumps to calculate the average height, and write the result on the board. (For example, if the first jump was 70 inches and the second jump was 74 inches, write *70 + 74 = 144 and 144 ÷ 2 = 72. The average height is 72 inches.*)

e. To figure out how high the jump would be on the moon, students must multiply the average height by six. Calculate the height of the "moon jump" for your volunteer's average height. (For example, the "moon jump" for an average height of 72 inches would be 432 inches.)

f. Teams then add the average heights of all of their jumps to find the total of their team's moon jumps. The team with the highest score wins.

5. Answer any questions, and then direct each team to find a wall where students will have enough room to jump. (If the classroom or hallway does not have enough empty wall space, take the class outdoors and let students work along the side of the school building. Make sure students are wearing the proper shoes.)

6. As students play the game, check that they measure the jumps accurately and that they are able to do the calculations correctly. Have them record the measurements on their reproducible.

7. After the game, ask teams to compare their scores. Then discuss the following questions to help students think about the effects of weaker gravity:

- *Suppose people could live on the moon. What kinds of sports or games would be easier to play on the moon than on Earth?* (activities that require people to jump high or to carry weights, such as basketball, high-jump competitions, weightlifting, and pole vaulting)
- *What kinds of sports or games would be more difficult to play on the moon than on Earth?* (activities that require objects to be weighed down or pulled down, such as bowling, hockey, and sledding)

978-1-4129-5930-8

Name _____ Date _____

Moon Jumps

Directions: Take turns jumping as high as you can.

Each time you jump:
1. Stick a piece of tape on the wall.
2. Measure the height of the tape. Record the number.
3. Do Steps 1 and 2 two times.
4. Add the two heights, then divide the sum by 2 to get the average height. Record the average height.
5. Multiply the average height by 6 to find out how high you would have jumped on the moon. Record that height.
6. Add all the "moon jumps" to get your team's total score.

Name	Height of First Jump	Height of Second Jump	Average Height (Divide the sum of the two jumps by 2)	"Moon Jump" (Multiply the average height by 6)
			Team's Total Score (Add the moon jumps)	

Solar System Word Bag

Objective

Students will demonstrate an understanding of terms related to the solar system.

A study of the solar system involves learning specific vocabulary. Use this game to help students review important facts and terms. Play the game when students are nearing the end of their solar system unit.

Materials
- 15 to 20 index cards
- paper lunch bag
- large paper clip
- music recording
- CD or cassette player

1. Ahead of time, select 15 to 20 vocabulary words related to your students' study of the solar system (see the list below), and write each word on an index card. Place the cards in a paper bag. Fold over the top of the bag twice, and secure it with a paper clip. Set the bag aside.

    Select terms from the following list, or use terms from your own curriculum materials.

Solar System Terms

asteroid: chunk of rock that moves around the sun

astronomer: scientist who studies objects in space

atmosphere: blanket of air that surrounds Earth

axis: imaginary line on which an object rotates

comet: ball of ice and dust that moves around the sun

constellation: group of stars that forms a pattern

crater: bowl-shaped pit

inner planets: the four planets closest to the sun

meteor: chunk of rock from space

meteorite: chunk of rock or metal that falls from space and hits Earth's surface

orbit: the path an object takes as it moves around another object in space; or the act of moving around another object

outer planets: the planets that are farthest from the sun

revolution: movement of an object around another object

rotation: spinning of an object on its axis

star: ball of hot, glowing gas

telescope: instrument that makes faraway objects look bigger

---

2. Write the term *solar system* on the board. Ask the class what the term means. Review the fact that the solar system is the sun and all the objects that move around it. Next, write the word *planet* on the board and ask for its meaning. Remind the class that a planet is a large body of rock or gas that travels around the sun.

3. Tell students that they are going to play a game to review their solar system vocabulary. Then direct the class to stand in a large circle. Have students call out *1, 2, 1, 2* in order to divide themselves into two teams.

4. Explain and model the rules of the game.
   a. When the music plays, students begin passing the bag of game cards around the circle.
   b. When the music stops, the student who is holding the bag opens it and draws a card. The student says the term written on the card and then gives a definition or a fact about that term. (For example, for the word *star*, the student might define the word as "a ball of hot, glowing gas" or state that the sun is the star closest to Earth.)
   c. If the student responds correctly, he or she keeps the card. If the student cannot state a definition or a fact, he or she puts the card back into the bag and clips it closed for the next round.
   d. At the end of the game, teams count how many cards they collected. The team with the most cards wins the game.

5. Play a few practice rounds to make sure students understand how to play. Then begin a real game.

6. After the game, have students use the words in sentences.

Extended Learning
Have students make a chart or a picture dictionary that highlights the terms they learned from their solar system unit.

CHAPTER 4

Social Studies

Autographs Around the World

Materials
• Autographs Around the
  World reproducible

Objective
Students will learn about the cultural backgrounds of their classmates.

The United States has one of the world's most diverse populations. People from many different countries and cultures have immigrated here. In this game, students learn about their classmates' cultural backgrounds as well as to appreciate one another's differences.

1. Ask students to stand if their parents or grandparents came to America from a different country. Count the standing students and write the number on the board. Next, ask students to stand if their great grandparents, great-great grandparents, or relatives even further back came here from another country. Finally, ask if there are any students who have Native American ancestors, and tell them to stand. All of your students should now be standing.

2. Ask each student to name at least one country from which his or her ancestors originated. List the countries on the board. Tell the class that the United States is made up of people from all over the world. Then tell students that they will be playing a game to learn about the various backgrounds of their classmates.

3. Give students a copy of the **Autographs Around the World reproducible (page 66)**. Point to the boxes on the page, and explain that each box contains a sentence about a person's background. Then call on various students to read the sentences aloud to the class.

4. Explain and model the rules of the game.
   a. At your signal, players move around the room asking one student at a time if a sentence in a box applies to him or her. If it does, that student signs the box. (For example, if Ryan asks Mina if she was born outside the United States and Mina says *yes*, then Mina signs the box with the sentence *I was born outside the United States*.)
   b. The goal of the game is to get an autograph, or signature, in every box. However, a student can sign a player's sheet only one time.

5. Invite several volunteers to help you model the game. Demonstrate asking if a statement applies to the volunteers and pretend to sign a student's game sheet. Tell the class that since you already signed that student's paper, you cannot sign it again. Answer any questions, and then have students play on their own.

6. Check to see that students understand the rules and that they are collecting only one autograph from each classmate.

7. After the game, ask students to return to their seats. Invite them to share what they found out about their classmates. For example, have students name a classmate who was born in the United States, one who was born outside of the United States, one whose parents immigrated to America, and so on.

8. Point out that your class represents a number of different cultures. Talk about the benefits that cultural diversity brings to a country like the United States.

Extended Learning

Ask the class to make a graph to illustrate information gathered during the game based on the following questions:

- *How many students in our class were born in the United States? How many were born outside of the United States?*

- *What languages are spoken by the students in our class?*

- *Which countries are represented by the students in our class?*

- *How many students speak only one language? How many speak two languages? How many speak three languages?*

Autographs Around the World

Name _Shana_

I was born in the United States.	I was born outside of the United States.	At least one of my parents came to America from a different country.	I can speak another language besides English.
Brett	Anna	Leah	Yuki
I have relatives who live outside of the United States.	The first language I spoke was English.	The first language I spoke was not English.	I can read or write in a language other than English.
Carlos	Shayne	Sohee	Maria
Both of my parents were born in the United States.	I eat mostly American foods.	My family usually eats meals different from most American meals.	My family sometimes watches TV shows that are not in English.
Jenny	Matt	Kruti	Daniel

66 Engage the Brain: Games • Grade 3   Reproducible   978-1-4129-5930-8 • © Corwin Press

Date _May 10, 2008_

Autographs Around the World

I can speak another language besides English.	I can read or write in a language other than English.	My family sometimes watches TV shows that are not in English.
At least one of my parents came to America from a different country.	The first language I spoke was not English.	My family usually eats meals different from most American meals.
I was born outside of the United States.	The first language I spoke was English.	I eat mostly American foods.
I was born in the United States.	I have relatives who live outside of the United States.	Both of my parents were born in the United States.

Lingo Bingo

Objective
Students will identify geography terms that match given definitions.

<table>
<tr><td>

Materials
- Lingo Bingo Game Cards reproducibles
- cardstock
- scissors
- paper lunch bag
- drawing paper
- counters or other game markers

</td></tr>
</table>

Bingo games are a fun way to review vocabulary, math facts, and other kinds of information that involve pairings (vocabulary terms with their meanings, addition problems with their sums, and so on). In Lingo Bingo, students play a Bingo game that reinforces their understanding of geography terms. Play the game after your students have been introduced to the terms.

1. Ahead of time, copy the **Lingo Bingo Game Cards reproducibles (pages 69–70)** on cardstock. Cut out the cards and place them in a paper bag.

2. Present a quick review of some of the geography terms that students have learned. Begin by writing *mountain* on the board. Have a student draw a picture to illustrate the term and give its definition. Next, call on other students to illustrate and define the terms *valley, bay,* and *canyon.*

3. Tell students that they will review the words they have learned in their geography lessons by playing Lingo Bingo. Distribute drawing paper and a handful of counters or other game markers to each student. Show students how to fold their paper in half crosswise twice, open up the paper, and then fold it in half lengthwise twice. When students unfold their paper, the fold lines form a 4 x 4 grid with 16 spaces.

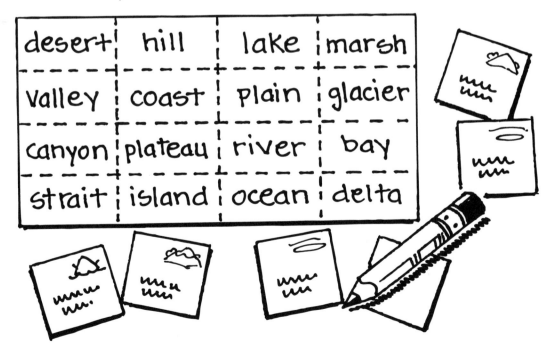

desert	hill	lake	marsh
valley	coast	plain	glacier
canyon	plateau	river	bay
strait	island	ocean	delta

4. Write the list of 24 terms on the board. Have students select 16 words from the list and write them randomly in their grid. Then explain and model the rules of the game.
   a. Draw a game card from the bag and read aloud the definition.
   b. Players name the corresponding geography term. Check off the word on the board.
   c. Players check if the word is on their grid. If they have the word, they put a counter on the corresponding space.
   d. The game continues with you drawing cards and calling out the definitions. The first player to cover four words in a row horizontally, vertically, or diagonally calls out: *Lingo Bingo!* The winner becomes the new caller for the next game.

5. Play a practice round with several game cards to make sure students understand how to play. Then begin the game. As students play, circulate around the room to make sure they are covering the correct words.

6. After the game, invite students to discuss other ways they can review words and their definitions. Ask them to offer suggestions for other content areas or subjects in which they can use the Lingo Bingo game for reviewing terms.

Extended Learning

Place the game materials and some drawing paper at a learning center. Have students play the game in small groups for additional practice.

978-1-4129-5930-8

Lingo Bingo Game Cards

Part of a lake or ocean with land around some of it (bay)	Deep valley with high, steep sides (canyon)	Narrow strip of land that juts out into a lake or sea (cape)	Land that is along a sea or ocean (coast)
Land that forms at the mouth of a river (delta)	Area of dry land that supports few plants (desert)	Large, slow-moving mass of ice (glacier)	Land covered mainly by grass and few trees (grassland)
Rounded land form that rises above the land around it (hill)	Land surrounded by water (island)	Narrow strip of land that joins two larger land areas (isthmus)	Body of water surrounded by land (lake)

Lingo Bingo Game Cards

Low, wet land (marsh)	Landform that rises high above the land around it (mountain)	Row of mountains (mountain range)	Place where a river empties into another body of water (mouth)

Large body of saltwater that covers 2/3 of earth's surface (ocean)	Area of land almost entirely surrounded by water (peninsula)	Area of flat, almost treeless land (plain)	Area of high, flat land with steep sides (plateau)

Large stream of water that flows into a lake or an ocean (river)	Narrow water passage that joins two larger bodies of water (strait)	Huge, treeless plain found in the Arctic (tundra)	Low land between hills or mountains (valley)

Reproducible   *978-1-4129-5930-8 •* © Corwin Press

American Symbols Q & A

Objective

Students will research facts about American symbols.

Research becomes more motivating and fun when students know that a game will be associated with it. In this activity, students look up information about patriotic symbols and use their research to create a question-and-answer game.

Materials
- American Symbols Question Cards reproducible
- cardstock
- scissors
- pictures of the American flag, Statue of Liberty, bald eagle, Liberty Bell, Uncle Sam, and Great Seal of the United States
- encyclopedias and library books about American symbols
- large sheets of drawing paper

1. Ahead of time, make six copies of the **American Symbols Question Cards reproducible (page 73)** on cardstock. Cut out the cards and put them into six separate piles according to the symbol on each card (i.e., all the flag cards in one pile, all the Statue of Liberty cards in another pile, and so on).

2. Display pictures of the American flag, the Statue of Liberty, a bald eagle, the Liberty Bell, Uncle Sam, and the Great Seal of the United States. Ask what these symbols have in common. Elicit from the class that these are all symbols of the United States. Explain that a country's symbols stand for ideas its citizens believe in, such as freedom and courage. Add that these symbols inspire people to view their country with pride.

3. Tell the class that American symbols have a rich history. Explain that they will be working in groups to research six important American symbols.

4. Divide the class into six groups, and assign each group a symbol from the reproducible. Tell students that later they will be playing American Symbols Q & A, a question-and-answer game based on the information they learn.

5. Give each group a set of six blank symbol cards (a different set for each group). Provide encyclopedias and library books for students to do their research. If computers are available, let students also look up information on the Internet. Encourage groups to find interesting facts and historical information about each symbol.

6. Have students write questions based on the information they find. Instruct them to write each question on the front of the card and the answer on the back. Encourage students to write a variety of questions. Write some examples on the board. For example, illustrate that a question about the stars on the U.S. flag can be posed in three different ways:
   - *What do the stars on the American flag stand for?* (50 states)
   - *How many stars are on the American flag—30, 50, or 65?* (50)
   - *True or False? The stars on the American flag stand for the presidents.* (false)

7. Provide ample time for students to work in their groups and write their questions. Walk around the room to check that students are finding the information they need and that they are writing clear, concise questions.

8. Collect the completed cards. Have students sit with their groups. Assign each group a number. Place the cards in separate piles on your desk. Then explain and model the rules of the game.
   a. Select a card from the first pile. The group who worked on that topic *cannot* answer the question. Read aloud the question.
   b. The first student who answers correctly scores a point for his or her team. If no one can answer, the group who worked on the card states the correct response.
   c. Continue selecting cards and reading questions. The team with the most points at the end of the game is the winner.

9. Read a few questions so students can play a practice round, and then begin the game.

10. As a follow-up, ask students to share a new fact they learned or something they found interesting about one of the symbols.

Extended Learning
Invite groups to make posters that illustrate what they learned about the symbols they researched.

American Symbols Question Cards

American Flag	Statue of Liberty
Bald Eagle	Liberty Bell
Uncle Sam	Great Seal of the United States

Fact or Fiction?

Materials
- social studies textbooks
- chart paper

Objectives
Students will research information in their textbooks.
Students will write true or false statements based on this information.
Students will challenge their classmates to distinguish true statements from false ones.

Third graders learn about communities and how they are run. In this game, students look through their social studies textbook for information on local, state, and federal governments.

1. Write the following sentences on the board:

   The leader of a state government is called a governor.
   The leader of a city government is called a governor.

   Tell the class that only one of the sentences is true. Challenge the class to spot the true sentence, and call on a student to underline it. (The first sentence is true.) Explain that a *governor* is head of the state government; the head of a city government, on the other hand, is called a *mayor*.

2. Inform students that they will be playing a game to help them learn more about government. Then instruct them to take out their social studies textbooks. Distribute writing paper to the class.

3. Encourage students to look through their textbooks for information about the government. Write the appropriate sections or pages on the board to guide students' research.

4. Tell students that they should list ten pairs of statements about the information they learned. One statement in each pair is true, while the other statement is false. Point to the statements you wrote at the beginning of the lesson as examples. Students will use their sentences to play a game in which players try to differentiate between true statements and false statements.

5. Provide enough time for students to read their textbooks and find appropriate material to write about. If any students have difficulty, have them read one or two paragraphs with you. Then ask them questions about what they've read to help clarify their thinking. They can then give you a factual statement regarding what they've read and make up a corresponding fictional statement. Examples include: *Both state and local governments collect taxes from citizens. Only the state government collects taxes from citizens.*

6. Divide the class into pairs. Then explain the rules of the game.
   a. Partners trade papers. Students read their partner's statements and underline the factual one in each pair.
   b. Students return their partner's paper. The students who wrote the statements score their partner's responses. Players earn one point for each factual statement they identified. The player with the highest score wins.

7. After the game, discuss what the class learned about American government. Write students' responses on chart paper. They will be amazed at the amount of material they were able to cover by reading and writing facts on their own!

Assembly-Line Relay

Materials

- new box of crayons
- long tables
- 25 to 30 plastic containers with lids
- shoe boxes (large enough to hold 5 plastic containers; 1 per team)
- bags of 15 cotton balls (1 bag per team)
- 2" x 3" sheets of white paper (5 per team)
- markers (1 per team)
- glue sticks (1 per team)

Objective

Students will demonstrate how assembly lines help manufacturing companies make products more efficiently.

Assembly lines have revolutionized the way products are manufactured. The following relay will help students see the efficiency in the assembly-line method of production.

1. Show students a box of crayons, and ask how they think the crayons were made and packaged. Tell students that crayons, like many other products, are produced in factories where workers use machines to make products quickly.

2. Explain that in a factory products are made in steps. In each step, the product is handled by certain workers. To make crayons, for example, some people work with heated wax to mold the crayons, others work with machines that wrap the hardened crayons, and still others work at placing various colored crayons into a box.

3. Discuss with students how factories can make products more quickly and easily than people who make products by hand. Tell the class that factories use machines that can do a great deal of work in a short period of time. In addition, factories use *assembly lines*. Explain that in an assembly line, different people work on specific jobs to produce the completed product.

4. Tell students that they are going to play a game called Assembly-Line Relay to help them see what it is like to work on an assembly line. Then divide the class into teams of five players each. (Some teams may have four players; the fourth player must then do the jobs of the fourth and fifth players.)

5. Place long tables at one end of the room. (You will need a table for each team.) Put a box of plastic containers without lids at the opposite end of the room, five for each table. Place the following materials in a line on each table: a bag of 15 cotton balls, five container lids, five paper labels, a glue stick, and a marker.

978-1-4129-5930-8

6. Assign each team to a table, and have team members line up along one edge.

7. Ask a team to demonstrate the following steps of the relay while you explain the rules:
   - Step 1: The first player (the one nearest the box of containers) runs to the box, picks up a container, runs back, and hands the container to the second player.
   - Step 2: The second player places three cotton balls in the container.
   - Step 3: The third player puts on the lid and then glues on a paper label.
   - Step 4: The fourth player uses the marker to write *cotton balls* on the label.
   - Step 5: The fifth player runs with the container to the box where the empty containers are kept and places it inside.

   The first team to "produce" five containers of cotton balls wins.

8. Answer any questions, and then begin the game. As teams race, monitor students to make sure that they understand what they need to do for their specific "jobs."

9. After the game, discuss the following questions:
   - *Did your task get easier the more often you performed it?*
   - *Why do you think an assembly line is used at factories?*
   - *How can you test which is faster—having one student do all five tasks or having an assembly line with a student assigned to each task?* (If there is time, invite students to test their ideas.)

Super-Duper Inventions

Materials
- Invention Cards reproducibles
- cardstock
- scissors
- cell phone

Objective
Students will identify inventions that have changed society and affected the way people live.

People have been inventing things for thousands of years. In the past 200 years, however, inventions and discoveries have had an incredible impact on society. This game presents some of these inventions and encourages students to think about how they have affected the way people live.

1. Ahead of time, copy the **Invention Cards reproducibles (pages 80–81)** onto cardstock. Cut out the cards and place them in a stack. Place the card that reads *telephone* on top.

2. Show students a cell phone. Ask them to share how often their families use phones. Tell the class that Alexander Graham Bell invented the telephone in 1876. Today there are phones in almost every home and building. Ask the class to name ways that life would be different if there weren't any phones (e.g., *people would not be able to call one another to talk; people would have to send written or typed messages instead*).

3. Tell the class that the telephone is one example of an invention that has greatly affected the way people work and live. Then have students brainstorm other inventions that have had an impact on society (e.g., *washing machine, stove, television, car, airplane, refrigerator, electricity, computer*).

4. Inform students that they are going to play a game in which they must give clues to their teams about certain inventions. Then divide the class into two teams. Explain and model the rules of the game.

    a. A player from the first team draws a game card from the pile. The player silently reads the card, which includes the name of an invention and target words that cannot be used as part of the clues.

    b. At your signal, the player gives clues about the invention. If the player uses a target word, the team's turn is over.

    c. If the team correctly names the invention within one minute, they keep the card. If the team cannot name the invention, the other team gets a chance to guess.

    d. Play continues with a player on the other team giving clues for a new invention.

    e. The team with the most cards at the end of the game wins.

5. Show the game card that reads *telephone*. Point out that the word at the top (in this case, *telephone* and *phone* are both acceptable) is the invention that players must guess. Next, point to the words below the invention's name. Explain that the player must not use those words (in this case, *talk*, *speak*, *call*, and *ring*) in his or her clues. Then have students brainstorm clues that a player might give in order to help his or her team (e.g., *You use this when you need to give somebody a message. It lets you hear the person's voice. It is found in most people's homes*).

6. Once students understand how to play, begin the game.

7. After the game, have students discuss other inventions that affect their lives. Ask them to tell how these items make their lives easier or better in some way.

Invention Cards

✂

telephone (or **phone**)	airplane (or **plane**)	radio
Don't use these words: • talk • speak • call • ring	Don't use these words: • air, airline • fly • flight • pilot	Don't use these words: • music • disc jockey • broadcast • station
train	automobile (or **car**)	television (or **TV**)
Don't use these words: • rail • railroad • tracks • caboose	Don't use these words: • auto • tires • windshield • ride	Don't use these words: • screen • channels • commercials • station
computer	clock	camera
Don't use these words: • mouse • e-mail • Internet • keyboard	Don't use these words: • watch • time • hour • minute	Don't use these words: • photo • photographer • picture • click

Invention Cards

bicycle (or **bike**)	**pencil**	**photocopier** (or **copier**)
Don't use these words: • wheels • pedal • handlebars • tricycle	Don't use these words: • pen • write • print • paper	Don't use these words: • photo • copy • pictures • Xerox™
refrigerator (or **fridge**)	**dishwasher**	**sewing machine**
Don't use these words: • cold • freeze • freezer • food	Don't use these words: • dishes • wash • detergent • plates	Don't use these words: • sew • clothes • machine • stitch
lightbulb	**washing machine**	**microwave oven** (or **microwave**)
Don't use these words: • light, bulb • screw • lamp • switch	Don't use these words: • wash • clothes • detergent • dryer	Don't use these words: • cook • oven • food • fast

CHAPTER 5

Physical Education, Art, and Music

Soccer Bowling

Materials
- 4 rubber balls
- 12 bowling pins or empty soda bottles weighted with rocks
- chalk

Objective
Students will practice kicking a ball and knocking down pins.

Running, hitting a target, and other typical P.E. activities help students develop large-muscle skills and hand-eye coordination. In this game, students practice kicking a ball and aiming at a target.

1. Ask students to describe the game of bowling. Elicit from them that bowling involves rolling a ball and knocking down pins. Tell students that they will be playing a different kind of bowling game.

2. Gather rubber balls, bowling pins (or 12 soda bottles weighted down with several rocks), and some chalk to draw lines on the pavement. Take the class outdoors to a large, open space on the playground.

3. Draw two parallel lines on the pavement about 15 to 20 feet apart. Arrange three pins in a row, midway between the two lines. Have students form two teams. Ask the teams to stand facing each other behind the two lines while you explain the rules. Invite six volunteers to help you demonstrate the game.
   a. The goal of the game is to kick the ball and knock down as many pins as possible.
   b. One team member places a ball on the ground and kicks it toward a pin. When the ball crosses the two lines, a student from the opposing team picks it up.
   c. Teams alternate kicking the ball and retrieving it.
   d. Players earn one point each time they knock down a pin. The players on each team take turns kicking the ball so that every player has an equal chance of scoring points. Teams keep track of their own points.
   e. The game ends when all the pins are knocked down. The team with the most points at the end of the game wins.

4. After the demonstration, divide the class into teams of six students. Mix up the teams so those students with previous soccer experience are spread out among the teams. Have each team then separate into two smaller teams. Then draw lines to designate a playing area for each team. Finally, invite students to play the game on their own.

5. Circulate around the playground to check that everyone understands how to play the game. If any teams are having difficulty hitting their targets, move players closer to the pins. On the other hand, if the teams are easily hitting their targets, move players farther from the pins.

6. After the game, gather the class together. Discuss the following questions to help students evaluate their learning:
   - *How did you select which pins to target?*
   - *Were you able to hit the target most of the time, half of the time, or less than half of the time?*
   - *Did your accuracy improve as you gained more practice?*
   - *What was the hardest part of the game?*

Tiptoe, Run!

Materials
• none

Objective

Students will walk quietly to the opposing team and, at a signal, try to run back to a designated area without getting tagged.

Tag games are fun and easy, plus they promote exercise and fitness. The following game is a twist on the traditional game of tag. Instead of having only one or two players being "It," an entire team takes on the role of the chaser.

1. Ask students to explain how to play tag. Have them point out that players who are "It" try to chase and tag others. Tell students that they will be playing a form of tag called Tiptoe, Run!

2. Take the class outdoors to a large, open area. Either the field or a paved area will do fine.

3. Divide the class into two teams. Designate a real or an imaginary line as "home" to each team. The lines should be at least 20 yards apart.

4. Explain and model the rules of the game.
   a. Team 1 stands on their line with their backs turned to Team 2. Team 2 stands on their line, facing Team 1.
   b. When you say *go,* Team 2 tiptoes quietly and quickly toward Team 1. Team 2's players must approach their opponents cautiously so that Team 1 cannot hear how close they are.
   c. When you say *run,* Team 2's players run back home while Team 1's players chase and try to tag them. Team 1's players try to tag as many players on Team 2 as possible.
   d. When Team 2 reaches home, count those players who were tagged. That number becomes Team 1's score.
   e. Teams switch roles and play again. The team with the highest score after several rounds wins the game.

5. Clarify the boundaries for the playing field, and point out any places where students should *not* run. Remind them how to play tag politely and with good sportsmanship: Tag only certain parts of the body, and do not push or shove when tagging.

6. Answer any questions, and then begin the game. Monitor students to make sure that they are running within the designated area.

7. After the game, ask students to suggest ways that they can change the game. Provide an example, such as having players walk backward or hop on one foot instead of tiptoe. Incorporate students' suggestions into future games.

Variation of the Game

The game begins the same way, but when Team 1 gives chase, any players who are caught become part of Team 1. Then have Team 1 line up again, with their backs turned to Team 2. Play another round, with Team 1 catching as many players as possible. The game continues until all, or almost all, of Team 2 has been "captured."

Artsy Scavenger Hunt

Materials

- Artsy Scavenger Hunt reproducible
- pictures featuring different elements of art
- objects with various textures
- paper or fabric samples featuring different shades and tints
- old magazines
- scissors
- butcher paper
- glue

Objective

Students will identify the elements of art in pictures.

Learning about the various elements of art helps students better understand and appreciate artwork. In this game, students go on a scavenger hunt in which they look for pictures that illustrate various art elements. Play the game after students have already been introduced to the different elements of art.

1. Show students a picture that features one or more art elements (e.g., a magazine picture that shows a repeating pattern or a photograph that shows different shades of a color), and discuss the elements with the class. Remind students that artists use basic elements of art to create their work. Explain that these elements include line, color, shape, texture, and pattern. List the elements on the board.

2. Show students a picture of a famous painting, such as Van Gogh's *Sunflowers*. Review the colors, lines, shapes, and textures featured in the artwork.

3. Tell students that they will be going on a scavenger hunt in which they look for pictures that illustrate the basic elements of art. Then give each student a copy of the **Artsy Scavenger Hunt reproducible (page 88)**.

4. Discuss each item on the page, and make sure that students understand each concept. Following are some suggestions:
   - Have volunteers draw lines on the board to illustrate different kinds of lines.
   - Use crayons or markers to provide examples of warm colors and cool colors.
   - Show paper or fabric samples that feature different shades and tints. Explain that shades are made by adding black to a color and tints are made by adding white.
   - Have volunteers draw designs on the board to illustrate how lines, colors, and shapes are used to make patterns.
   - Ask volunteers to draw shapes on the board to show what geometric, irregular, and symmetrical shapes look like.
   - Show students objects with different textures (e.g., a sheet of sandpaper, a cotton ball, a hairbrush).

5. Divide the class into small groups, and give each group several magazines and scissors. Explain and model the rules of the game.

   a. Groups look through magazines for pictures that fit the categories on the reproducible.

   b. Students cut out the pictures and check off the corresponding items on their list.

   c. The group that checks off the most items wins the game.

6. Model flipping through a magazine. Think aloud about different pictures and the categories they illustrate. Then point out pictures and invite volunteers to identify which categories they could check off. Once students have a good understanding of what to look for, begin the game.

7. As a follow-up, have groups share their pictures. Ask questions such as: *What was used to make that pattern? How many shades or tints of green do you see in that picture? What kinds of lines do you see? Are these colors warm or cool?*

Extended Learning

Have group members glue their pictures to a sheet of poster paper. Instruct students to label which element each picture illustrates. Display the posters on a bulletin board.

Artsy Scavenger Hunt

Directions: Find pictures that show the different art elements listed below. Check off the items as you find them.

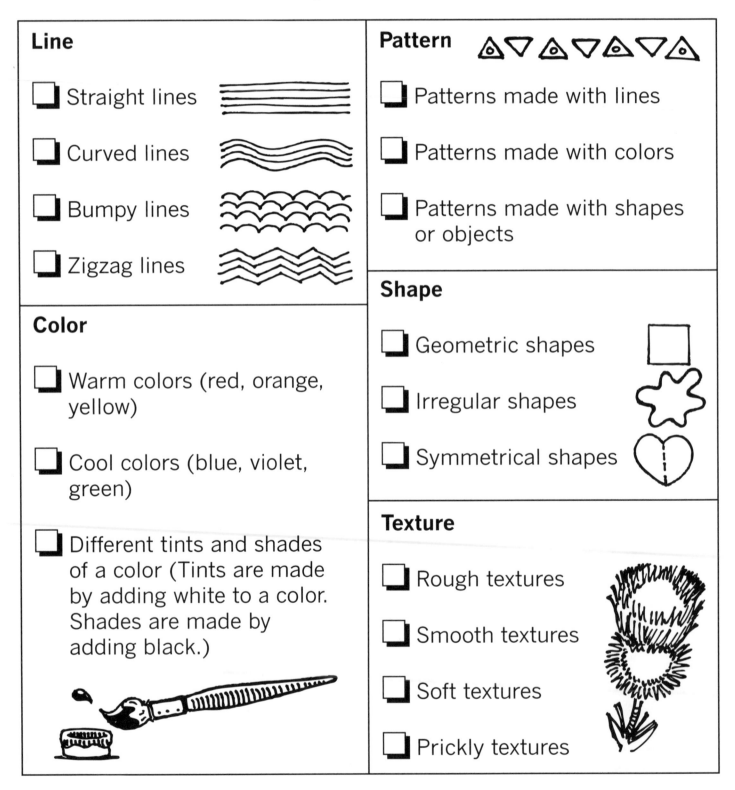

Line

☐ Straight lines

☐ Curved lines

☐ Bumpy lines

☐ Zigzag lines

Color

☐ Warm colors (red, orange, yellow)

☐ Cool colors (blue, violet, green)

☐ Different tints and shades of a color (Tints are made by adding white to a color. Shades are made by adding black.)

Pattern

☐ Patterns made with lines

☐ Patterns made with colors

☐ Patterns made with shapes or objects

Shape

☐ Geometric shapes

☐ Irregular shapes

☐ Symmetrical shapes

Texture

☐ Rough textures

☐ Smooth textures

☐ Soft textures

☐ Prickly textures

Blindfold Creations

Objective

Students will make drawings without using their sense of sight. As they draw, they will use spatial perception and visual memory to complete their pictures.

Materials
- index cards
- 2 blindfolds
- clock or watch with second hand

We rely heavily on our sense of sight when we draw. However, if that sense is taken away, we need to use our other senses to help make the drawing. In this game, students try to draw recognizable pictures while wearing a blindfold.

1. Ahead of time, write the names of animals and objects on index cards. Choose simple items that students should be able to draw (e.g., cup, book, cat, mouse). Make 10 to 15 word cards.

2. Call on a volunteer to draw a dog on the board. Point out that the student is able to draw fairly quickly.

3. Blindfold the student, and ask him or her to draw a second dog. Guide the class to notice how much more difficult the task becomes when the student cannot see.

4. Ask students why being blindfolded affects their ability to draw. Responses might include: *We cannot see where we are drawing lines. We cannot connect lines properly to form the picture.*

5. Tell students that they are going to play a game that challenges them to draw while blindfolded. As they draw, they should reflect on what they are doing and thinking in order to make their pictures as accurate as possible.

6. Divide the class into two teams. Place the word cards in a pile. Invite a volunteer to model the game as you explain the rules.
   a. A player from Team 1 comes to the board and chooses a word card from the stack. The player silently reads the word.
   b. Blindfold the student and remind players that only members of Team 1 can try to guess the object being drawn.
   c. When you say *go*, the player starts drawing a picture to help his or her team identify the word.
   d. If Team 1 guesses the word within 30 seconds, they score one point. If not, Team 2 gets a chance to name the word; however, they will not score any points.
   e. The game continues with teams taking turns reading word cards and drawing pictures. The team with the most points wins the game.

7. Have another volunteer draw clues for a new word, and invite the class to identify the word. Once students have a good understanding of how to play, begin a real game.

8. After the game, ask students who drew the pictures to share their responses to the following questions:
   - *Because you could not see, what did you do to try to form the picture?* (For example, did students try to "see" the picture in their mind? Did they pay more attention to the lines they were forming as they drew? Did they avoid lifting their hand from the board?)
   - *Why does drawing while blindfolded make you more aware of the lines you are forming?* (For example, students have to think carefully about the length and direction of each line because they cannot see them.)

Variation of the Game

Have students play the game with a partner. Ask them to draw on paper instead of the board.

978-1-4129-5930-8

Squiggle Art

Objective

Students will create imaginative drawings from preexisting lines.

Materials
• Squiggle Art Cards reproducible
• scissors

Art activities are ideal for developing imagination and sparking creativity. In this game, students work with a partner to create interesting pictures from simple lines.

1. Draw a squiggly line on the board. Ask the class how they might turn the line into a picture. Call on a volunteer to come to the board and make a picture with the line. For example, the student might draw a caterpillar or a decorative picture frame.

2. Draw a zigzag line on the board. Call on a second volunteer to make a picture with the line. Ask students to suggest other ideas for using the line.

3. Tell students that they will be playing a game in which they make pictures from simple lines. Then divide the class into pairs, and give each pair a copy of the **Squiggle Art Cards reproducible (page 92)**. Instruct each pair to cut out the cards.

4. Explain and model the rules of the game.
   a. When you say *go*, partners work together to make each "squiggle" into a picture. Partners may work on one picture together, or they may complete separate pictures.
   b. After five minutes, partners count how many pictures they finished.

5. Answer any questions, and then begin the game. Circulate among students to make sure they understand the activity. If they are unable to make a picture with one line, have them move on to the next card.

6. After the game, ask students to choose two of their most interesting pictures to color. Display those pictures on a decorative bulletin board.

Name _____ Date _____

Squiggle Art Cards

Reproducible

Music Puzzler

Objective

Students will listen to a musical recording and identify as many instruments as possible.

Several musical instruments are often played together to produce a pleasing composition. In this game, students learn to distinguish and appreciate the sounds made by different musical instruments.

Materials
- pictures of musical instruments
- 2 or more musical instruments
- chart paper
- musical recording that features various instruments
- CD or cassette player

1. Show students pictures of various musical instruments. Help them to identify each instrument. If possible, show some actual instruments (such as rhythm instruments or a guitar and a flute) and play them briefly for the class. Point out the distinct quality of each sound. Explain that how an instrument is played affects its sound.

2. Tell students that there are four main groups of instruments. Point to your pictures or instruments as you discuss each type.
   - **Stringed Instruments:** The player either draws a bow back and forth over the strings or plucks the strings (violin, viola, cello, bass, harp, guitar).
   - **Wind Instruments:** The player blows through a tube (flute, clarinet, trumpet, trombone, saxophone).
   - **Percussion Instruments:** The player shakes or strikes the instrument (drum, triangle, xylophone).
   - **Keyboard Instruments:** The player presses keys (piano, organ, accordion).

3. Ask students to name some of the musical instruments they have heard live (at school concerts, parades, and so on) or recorded (on CDs, in movies, or on the radio). Point out that many musical instruments are played together in order to produce a pleasant sound. Create a chart that features the pictures of the instruments. Label each picture so students can refer to the chart during the game.

4. Tell students that they are going to play a game to see how well they can distinguish the sounds of different instruments. Then explain and model the rules of the game.
   a. Play a musical recording.
   b. Players listen carefully and write the names of any instruments they hear. If players do not know the name of a specific instrument, they can write the type of instrument or the instrument family (e.g., *stringed, wind, percussion,* or *keyboard*).
   c. After the game, list the instruments from the recording on the board. Players earn one point for each instrument they identified correctly. The player with the most points wins the game.

5. Have students close their eyes while you play a recording featuring one of the instruments. Ask them to name the instrument. Guide students to refer to the class chart if they need help with the name. Then begin the game. If you wish, darken the room or let students close their eyes to help them concentrate more fully on the music.

6. After the game, review the answers with the class. (Look at the CD or cassette cover; it will most likely list the instruments that were played.) List the instruments on the board.

7. As a follow-up, play the recording again, and have students see if they can hear the instruments they missed the first time.

Name That Song!

Objective

Students will identify a familiar song based on a line of lyrics.

Materials
• sentence strips

A game can make music time even more lively and fun! In this game, challenge students to look at lines from songs and identify the corresponding song titles.

1. Ahead of time, write short phrases from 15 to 20 songs on sentence strips. Choose songs with which students are familiar. For example, besides new songs that your class has learned at school, you might also choose well-known songs such as "The Star-Spangled Banner" and "Row, Row, Row Your Boat." Make the letters large enough so the entire class will be able to read the words when you hold up the sentence strips.

2. Ask students to name some of the songs they have learned at school. Then tell them that they will be playing a game to see how quickly they can recognize lyrics from familiar songs.

3. Divide the class into two teams. Explain and model the rules of the game.
   a. Hold up a sentence strip.
   b. Players read the phrase and name the corresponding song title. The first player to call out the correct title earns one point for his or her team.
   c. The team with the most points at the end of the game wins.

4. Display several phrases, and have students play a practice round. Then begin a real game.

5. After the game, invite students to suggest lines from other familiar songs to use for a future game.

References

Alsop, F. J. (2002). Bird. In *World book encyclopedia* (Vol. 2, pp. 332–329). Chicago, IL: World Book.

Badders, W., Bethel, L., Fu, V., Peck, D., et al. (2000). Sun, Moon, and Earth. *DiscoveryWorks 3* (pp. B6–B57). Boston, MA: Houghton Mifflin.

Beyers, J. (1998). The biology of human play. *Child Development, 69*(3), 599–600.

Bjorkland, D. F., & Brown, R. D. (1998). Physical play and cognitive development: Integrating activity, cognition, and education. *Child Development, 69*(3), 604–606.

Boehm, R. G., Hoone, C., McGowan, T. M., McKinney-Browning, M. C., et al. (2002). *Communities* (pp. A14–A15). Orlando, FL: Harcourt.

Caine, R. N., & Caine, G. (1994). *Making connections: Teaching and the human brain.* Menlo Park, CA: Addison-Wesley.

Chalupnik, J. D. (2002). Lever. In *World book encyclopedia* (Vol. 12, pp. 217–218). Chicago, IL: World Book.

Farndon, J. (1992). Rocks and soil. *How the earth works* (pp. 73–75). London, England: Dorling Kindersley.

Frank, M. S., Jones, R. M., Krockover, G. H., et al. (2000). *Harcourt science grade 3* (pp. B2–B57, C58–C89, E28–E43). Orlando, FL: Harcourt.

Gardner, H. (1983). *Frames of mind: The theory of multiple intelligences.* New York, NY: Basic Books.

Gibbons, J. W. (2002). Amphibian. In *World book encyclopedia* (Vol. 1, pp. 430–449). Chicago, IL: World Book.

Gorenstein, P. (2002). Moon. In *World book encyclopedia* (Vol. 13, p. 788). Chicago, IL: World Book.

Huey, R. B., & Wilson, W. H. (2002). Animal. In *World book encyclopedia* (Vol. 1, pp. 473–487). Chicago, IL: World Book.

Jensen, E. (2001). *Arts with the brain in mind.* Alexandria, VA: Association for Supervision and Curriculum Development.

Longyear, R. M. (2002). Music. In *World book encyclopedia* (Vol. 13, pp. 948–950). Chicago, IL: World Book.

McCarthy, B. (1990). Using the 4MAT system to bring learning styles to schools. *Educational Leadership, 48*(2), 31–37.

Means, D. B. (2002). Reptile. In *World book encyclopedia* (Vol. 16, pp. 250–252). Chicago, IL: World Book.

National Council for the Social Studies. (2002). *Expectations of excellence: Curriculum standards for social studies.* Silver Spring, MD: National Council for the Social Studies (NCSS).

National Council of Teachers of English and the International Reading Association. (1996). *Standards for the English language arts.* Urbana, IL: National Council of Teachers of English (NCTE).

National Council of Teachers of Mathematics. (2005). *Principles and standards for school mathematics.* Reston, VA: National Council of Teachers of Mathematics (NCTM).

National Research Council. (1996). *National science education standards.* Washington, DC: National Academy Press.

Rausch, J. (2003, November 12). *Spelling linked with word study.* Retrieved June 14, 2007, from the Inside WSU Web site: http://webs.wichita.edu/dt/insidewsu/show/article.asp?282.

Tate, M. L. (2003). *Worksheets don't grow dendrites: 20 instructional strategies that engage the brain.* Thousand Oaks, CA: Corwin Press.

Van de Walle, J. A. (2004). Developing measurement concepts. *Elementary and middle school mathematics: Teaching developmentally* (pp. 316–319). Boston, MA: Pearson Education.

Walpole, B. (1988). Movement. *175 science experiments to amuse and amaze your friends* (p. 94). New York, NY: Random House.

Wolfe, P. (2001). *Brain matters: Translating research into classroom practice.* Alexandria, VA: Association for Supervision and Curriculum Development.